ABERGAVENNY
in the Twentieth Century

ABERGAVENNY
in the Twentieth Century

ABERGAVENNY CIVIC SOCIETY

ABERGAVENNY
CIVIC SOCIETY

Published 1992 by

COMMA INTERNATIONAL

Lower Coed Morgan

Nr. Abergavenny, Gwent

Tel: 0873 840256

British Library Cataloguing in Publication Data

A catalogue record for this book is available
from the British Library

ISBN 0 9513977 4 5

Designed and Produced by Images Design and Print Ltd

Printed and Bound in Great Britain by Hartnolls Ltd, Bodmin, Cornwall.

DEDICATION

To the people of Abergavenny,
past, present and future.

CONTENTS

ACKNOWLEDGEMENTS

A book of this nature would not be possible without the combined efforts of a number of people. Firstly, the members of the Civic Society themselves, who have been so supportive and generous towards what must have seemed a very ambitious project; secondly, the book committee who assembled the material, who conducted interviews and a thousand other tasks often at the expense of much of their own time and energy. Particular thanks must go the contributors, not only to those whose names are listed in the book, but to others who sent information and whose material, in the end, was not selected for publication.

We are extremely grateful to Mrs Marjorie Stinchcome, whose charming sketches have added so considerably to the overall interest of the book. Anita Hill for the designing which has gone into the book. Mr Frank Olding, Curator of the Abergavenny Museum, contributed a number of photographs of the town in mid-century, and Mr P. W. Ellis and Mrs C. Marsh of the Gwent County Library have supplied us with copies of the comprehensive Bibliography of Gwent, together with a supplement relating to Abergavenny and District. Dick Merton Jones, Patrick Humphreys and Anita Hill supplied photographs of the town as it appeared in 1992 and Albert Lyons kindly let us make use of his collection of photographs from a much earlier period.

Finally, a special note of gratitude must go to Alwynne Fuller, the 1992 Hon. President of the Civic Society, who has steered the project through to completion, and who exercised her considerable skill of leadership and and diplomacy to achieve it, not to mention her apparently inexhaustible reserves of energy. It is safe to say that the book is in itself a testimonial to her period as a distinguished President.

Abergavenny Civic Society

Publications Sub-Committee:

Alwynne Fuller

Dick Merton-Jones

Pam Heath

Judy Foden

Howard Pullan

Patrick Humphreys

Brian Giles

Margaret Giles

INTRODUCTION

It has been a great pleasure and privilege to have been asked to put together this book for the Abergavenny Civic Society. Originally a rather haphazard collection of reminiscences of residents and former residents it progressed intermittently and through several hands with no very clear picture of what it was hoped it would become. An inspection revealed that what had been accumulated covered nearly the entire twentieth century and chronicled a period of change in the town unparalleled in previous ages.

The medieval market town of Abergavenny with its priory and castle, commanding the strategic valley of the Usk in its passage from the Welsh mountains to the coast at Newport, has long been known as the "Gateway of Wales". Its early history and close association with the Nevill family from the time of Henry VIII has received the attention of very many historians. Fortunately, some of the early structures of the past still survive, though many have been lost.

At the beginning of the twentieth century Abergavenny was a moderately important railway town, with three stations and three companies providing human and commercial transport throughout South Wales. It is fascinating to see from a street directory of the time, how many men were employed on the railways before the 1914-1918 war. Besides the railways horses were the primary means of locomotive power and there were about six blacksmiths and two veterinary practices in the town to cater for their needs.

The physical changes in the town have been enormous. Many fine buildings have been allowed to get into disrepair and have been pulled down, often highly insensitively, with nothing of value saved for future generations. In the 1950s there was a general vogue for wholesale clearance of districts with the result that streets of perfectly good houses were bulldozed and nothing much put in their place. Where the old houses escaped this fate they have been restored and still serve as useful and comfortable dwellings today.

Original Cottage Hospital, Castle Street.

Some of the business premises that were erected at about that time do not blend happily with any of the old buildings around them, as the Post Office and Employment Office illustrate all too clearly. We have been able to obtain pictures of three successive Abergavenny hospitals, ranging from what seems hardly more than a dispensary in Castle Street, followed by the Cottage Hospital in Hereford Road to the great modernistic Nevill Hall Hospital, which though modest in size by hospital standards today nevertheless, has one of the finest reputations for medical and nursing care in the country.

Much of the old industry of Abergavenny is no more; the Mills, the Tanneries and the Wool Merchants have all joined those trades whose operations have been centralised at one or two sites in Great Britain. Instead of railways, the internal combustion engine, a curious rarity at the start of the book, has come to dominate the appearance and structure of the town. As by-pass succeeds by-pass with yet more by-passes to succeed them one wonders if the worship of the car and lorry may not have gone too far in terms of destruction of neighbourhoods, pollution and aesthetic degradation, because it would appear that to own a motor vehicle is to drive it as much as possible with as little patience as is attributed to most race-tracks.

The Old Duke Inn next to the original hospital in Castle Street.

17

Abergavenny has had mixed fortune with the Planning authorities, which have been mostly at county or district level. We can be thankful that one County Planning Officer, the controversial late James Kegie, saw the Market towns of Monmouthshire as entities in themselves and not as suburbs of Birmingham or Cardiff as was proposed at one period. He felt expansion of such places as Monmouth, Usk and Abergavenny should be restricted so as to keep them within a human scale.

This concept was broken disastrously by the Monmouth District Council, against the advice of their own Technical Officers (and incidentally Abergavenny Civic Society), in the inexcusable siting of the turkey processing factory outside the natural boundary of the town and on land sloping down to the river Usk. There has already been one pollution incident there and others are always a possibility, especially as the plant gets older.

One thing that impressed me as I read the contributions is how little some things change in spite of physical appearances. Abergavenny has always been a good place to live in and grow up in. The late Peter Coleman's almost lyrical account of his childhood in the middle of the century and Charles Price's stories of "characters" of the town in his youth earlier on are accounts of a town where people and places mattered. We have no reason to believe that much has altered in that respect.

We are apt to think that drunken teenagers and fighting on Saturday nights are all symptomatic of our modern degenerate times, but Charles Price's tale of a battle in St John's Square in the 1920s makes one realise that *plus ca change plus c'est la même chose.*

It is remarkable that some societies such as the Cricket Club and Opera and Dramatic Societies have lasted for much more than a century, and look like thriving well into the twenty-first century at least.

We have illustrated some of the most modern buildings and some of the older ones which have been sensitively restored. The most dispiriting thing about the modern buildings is not their appearance, much of which seems quite acceptable and on an appropriate scale, but the (now) old-fashioned signs and logos which deface them. Commercial garages and supermarkets do not seem to have advanced from the 1960s in this respect, using labels designed over thirty years ago on today's structures.

For various reasons we have not been able to make use of every contribution that we have received and we have had to use a fairly strict editorial blue pencil to avoid possible libel suits from the descendants of some of the characters so graphically described. If this has the effect of watering down the reputations of some of them, I can only think we have done a service to their memory!

The text should be read in conjunction with the pictures. There are doubtless many omissions and if anyone would like to collect a second lot of reminiscences of Abergavenny I am sure they would be well received – but *please* let them come clearly typed and with photography of excellent quality only!

Patrick Humphreys

June 1992

G. A. HILL

The old Ferry boat which plied across the river at Llanwenarth no longer exists, except for a steel support which held one end of the wire hawser which was wound round by hand from the opposite side of the river. This was used chiefly by workmen who walked to Govilon station to catch the trains for various pits and steel works in the valleys. The charges were one penny per person and a halfpenny for cycles. The customers had to shout across the river to gain his attention.

In Castle Street next to the old school was the Animal Pound into which any straying animals would be "impounded" until claimed by their owners. A small fee would be charged according to the length of time the animal had been there. All these buildings and the old barn have been demolished by the "M.C.C.".

The town had two "Pop factories", one on the site of the Park Road Men's Conservative Club, and the other in Baker Street where Richards' Car Park is situated.

They used the old glass bottles with the marble in the neck to keep the contents intact.

At the rear of Morgan and Evans, the grocers in Cross Street (now Keylocks), was a candle factory. The whole of the manufacturing was done by hand power.

Annual outing for the railwaymen

There were three Cab ranks, one where the War Memorial now stands, one outside St Mary's Church, and one at the junction of Brecon and Merthyr Road. Each had an octagonal hut with a stove in which the cabbies would shelter and "Brew up". The most popular was the Memorial site which had a Public house, The Butcher's Arms (now demolished), nearby. Eventually

22

Motor Taxis took over, and the first in town was owned by Mr Baker, The White Horse Inn (opposite Barclays Bank). One of the many million Model T Fords.

In the yard adjoining the Radio repair shop in Brecon Road was a Monumental Masons display area, owned by Basil Evans, and behind was a Bakery owned by a Mr Gould.

The "Bike It" shop was a guest house, kept by Miss Cumming and Mrs Scattergood, so also was the Abergavenny Pet Shop in St Michael's Road. Beyond which was the Abergavenny Thursdays Football ground, now a Council House estate.

The Brecon Road Betting Shop was a grocers kept by "Binkey" Lewis, rather on the lines of the television series "Open All Hours". Opposite on the other side of the road was Mark Fine the Pawnbroker, the three Golden Balls hanging outside was the trade sign for such premises.

A few doors further was an old Chapel converted into the Old Constitutional Club. This closed when the new club was built in Park Road.

Further on was a Taxidermist shop kept by Mr E. Dalafield, regretfully now demolished.

Welsh lambs on their way to market.

Next to the club was a Jeweller's shop owned by a Mr Berkley. This later became an Antique shop, run by the two sons of the Pawnbroker, Leo and Ruben Fine.

Next to the "Bike It" shop was a shoe shop kept by Joe Norton who repaired boots and *made* them on the premises. He also had a battery charging plant for wireless sets and had his name outside the shop illuminated by an electric flashing sign, which created unusual interest as it was the first of its kind in the town. He also had a fine voice and was much in demand for local concerts.

Dr Tom Lloyd lived at Woodstock on the corner of Regent Street before he moved to Pen-y-Pound. It later became a nursing home, where I had my tonsils removed as a child.

Adjoining Woodstock was Foster & Hill's yard, the building business was started by Foster Brothers in 1860 and was one of the oldest established firms in the county.

An imposing public house named The George preceded Richards Stores. In their warehouse in the rear, opening off Baker Street, was a garage run by Mr Howard who built a three-wheeled motor car. Unfortunately owing to lack of finance and confidence

25

in his vehicle, only one was produced.

The shop next the Britannia Inn was kept by a French lady, and adjoining were several cottages, now shops.

On the right hand corner of White Horse Lane, opposite Barclays Bank, was the public house which gave its name to the Lane. Next door but one to the Bank was another inn called the Griffin. On the same side on the corner of Lewis' Lane was the King David, now Raynor the Optician.

Where Fine Fare now stands was a Butchers shop, and at the rear was a meat pie factory owned by Davy Williams. His pies were famous for many miles around.

On the site of Montague Burtons was Piper's Penny Bazaar, it later moved to the corner of Market Street, now Furnells Radio shop. The site was redeveloped and became a garage, with show rooms through to Nevill Street and Petrol pumps – hand operated – in the High Street owned by a Mr Westwood.

Immediately opposite – now Curry's – was Z. Wheatley, Jeweller, who was four times Mayor of the town during the first war.

Mr Daniels "High Class Tailor and Outfitter – Male and Female" had two large shops, one each side of the Market entrance. Lower down the road past Lloyds Bank was the Post Office, it later moved to Frogmore Street and remained there for fifty years, before moving again to its present site in St John's Square.

Opposite on the other side was the Wheatsheaf Inn, and next door but one was The White Swan Inn, both now shops.

The site of W.H. Smith used to be the Capital and Counties Bank, and next door was a coach-building firm, which in due time became Moon's Garage. Opposite on the other side of the road, was the Wellington Inn – now Dominic's. The town had over forty public houses, and all were proud of their "Good Stabling". On market days all the traps and carts would be parked outside, with the shafts of one pushed under the body of the other to save space in the road.

In Tudor Street on the river side of the road was the Old Volunteers Drill Hall which was used as a furniture store and antiques. Nearly opposite lived a family called Knight who kept a small shop. The son left the town when he grew up, and later became Lord Mayor of West Bromwich.

Frogmore Street, Abergavenny.

In Park Road the Tesco Garden Centre was the site of a Roller Skating Rink, later to become Jones Bros. garage.

Before Park Crescent was developed some of the land immediately adjoining the boundary of the Convent was known as the Athletic ground which was surrounded by a galvanized sheet fence. It was much used during holiday times.

In the 1930s Bertram Mills circus was an annual visitor to the Park. The whole show came by train to the Great Western Station, and road hauled from there.

In the 1920s Sir Alan Cobham brought his "Flying Circus" which operated from land which had been part of the old racecourse. Some of the forward looking council wanted to promote an airport on the site, but the old diehards said flying was only for the armed forces, and rich people. It would never be for the ordinary man in the street!

Situated in Union Road was the town's Workhouse, a gaunt stark, gloomy grey stone building darkened by the constant smoke from the railway sheds adjoining. Inhabited by the unfortunate people who had no alternative ruled over by the Board of Guardians who were elected by the public.

Old and new transport before the First World War.

Within the shadows of this unhappy place stood Nevill Hall, one of the seats of the Marquis of Abergavenny surrounded by all that His Grace could desire.

N.B. The Manager of Barclay's Bank held a record period of management at one bank. About twenty-five years, a Mr Britten, tall and most distinguished man, he took great pride in his greenhouse tomatoes and garden. Of his own will, he refused promotion in order to stay where he was so happy and content.

In Tudor Street there were some terrible slum properties, the worst being in what were called Courts. These consisted of an ally perhaps fifteen to twenty feet wide, and tenements on either side with a communal outside stand pipe for water. Accommodation would be one down and one up, with outside lavatories perhaps two to a Court of some twenty people. Here they existed in indescribable poverty and misery. Owing to the narrowness of the alley, one side was always in the shadow of the sun. Their only joy in life was the thought of death to remove them from such squalor.

DONALD WILLIAMS

In retrospect, the weather was always sunny and bright when we were young and the winters cold, rather more defined seasons than is the case now, or perhaps it is because one is older. At any rate, the roads were dusty and as horses were the principle means of transport, much less crowded than is the case nowadays.

The water cart was much in evidence in those days. During the hot weather, this horse-drawn vehicle arrived in town with its large tank, from which the driver could control the spray of water to lay the dust.

I am reminded too of the Blacksmith's shop and forge which was sited at the junction of Victoria street and Merthyr road. Here, it was of interest to see the smith shoeing the horses, acrid smoke and smell as the shoe was fitted to the foot of the horse. As a small boy I was much concerned as regards the pain that I imagined the horse was suffering although I never saw any evidence of that. In those days, the bowling of hoops was an interesting pastime, and the smith would make and repair our hoops when they became broken. It was fascinating to see him take the iron hoop and place it in the fire and produce a hot hearth to make the hoop ends white hot and sparkling. At the critical time, he would remove the hoop from the fire and hammer the broken ends together to weld them, and charge us a penny or twopence for the service. There was little risk of being "run over" in those days when running along the road bowling the hoop.

I recall with affection the memories of Park Street School, where Miss Clarke, a gentle and bird-like little lady was headmistress. To assist her was Miss Hanratty, who I remember as a strict disciplinarian, and of whom we were in great awe. Our favourite teacher was Miss Dolly Jones who subsequently became Mrs Reg Harry.

Growing a year or so older, we spent much time during the warmer weather in bathing in the river. This was out at Llanwenarth, crossing the field beyond the church. Just across the field adjacent to the river, there was a small orchard, and we used to "scrump" apples there, and I recall one day when Billie Vaughan who lived in Govilon was eating an apple while in the water when he was pushed accidentally, a piece of apple stuck in his throat and he fell under the water. Fortunately he was helped almost immediately and apart from fright he was soon all right. It might easily have been something of a tragedy though, and the orchard rather lost its charm for some of us.

Rother House Number '11' Nevill Street, Georgian House with splendid Adam style doorway.

In those early Edwardian days, sheep and cattle having changed hands in the market were usually driven through the main street via Lion street and Frogmore street to the railway goods yard in Brecon road. It was a weekly sight to see flocks of sheep and cows being driven by a drover armed with a stick and loud voice. Occasionally, an animal would prove to be awkward, and I recall the case of a heifer turning into Pen-y-Pound and finishing up in the playing field adjacent to the Grammar School. The poor beast, pursued by an excited drover, careered madly round the field finally charging at the railings at the far side. This had the effect of sobering the animal down and it was finally walked away after what had been a very exciting affair so far as we boys were concerned. In this connection, I remember my mother telling me of the occasion when a cow, instead of turning down into Frogmore street from Lion street, turned up into the High street and finished in Jones the china shop at the junction of St John's street and the High street. It must have given rise to the old saying "a bull in a china shop".

The Great Western Railway introduced one of the first bus services in the country which ran from Abergavenny to Brecon. This was introduced, I believe, in about 1906, and finally ran as a once daily service. The vehicle was a Milne Daimler petrol engined double decker bus with a stairway leading from the lower to the upper deck. Other than by horse this was the only means of travelling to Crickhowell and Brecon in those days. There was however, a horse drawn wagon operated by Evans, the carriers, and I once was given a ride to Crickhowell when I was about seven years of age. This was quite an adventure, and I found the experience thrilling.

A little Italian used to entertain shoppers in the main street on a hurdy-gurdy which was drawn by a donkey. On top of the hurdy was a green budgerigar in a cage. The little bird would take a card from a pack if the Italian was given a penny. I can see the even now, turning away at the wheel controlling the music roll and playing the repetitive tunes *ad nauseum*. In the hot summer weather, the organ would be replaced by an ice-cream float pulled by the same little donkey, and from which one could buy a cornet of ice-cream for a penny.

A notorious character in those days was "Ben". He earned a living by odd jobs which included cattle droving. So, on Tuesday, the big day of the week for him I suppose, he would repair to one of the pubs after his work was finished, and proceed to get absolutely as drunk as a coot. Unable to hold his liquor, he would become abusive and violent, so that the police would be called in to take him off to the station, and ultimately to Usk or wherever. This was a very frequent happening, so much so that Gobbanium who wrote a column for the *Chronicle* (he was in fact *the Chronicle*) could almost regard him as his best customer.

Derelict Houses

Former derelict houses restored.

The Abergavenny Amateur Operatic Society was an organisation which provided the Borough with annual performances of the Gilbert and Sullivan operas, the high spot of the season being the last night of the weekly run. The performance was invariably free and most professional as no doubt throughout the week apprehensions had dissipated and the show went with a swing, culminating in the presentation of bouquets.

Altogether a very colourful spectacle. The musical director for many years was A.L. Carr, a professional teacher of music, a couple of the cast's mainstays being Llew Evans and George Watts. The latter had an excellent tenor voice, and I can recall that two favourite items from his repertoire were "Take a pair of sparkling eyes" from *The Gondoliers* and "Because" a well known and loved ballad of the period. George sang these with great gusto and most pleasingly. Happy memories.

During the Great War of 1914-1918, the town became a camp for soldiers who trained in civil engineering, such as the construction of trenches of various types, underground shelters, redoubts and earth works of all kinds, as well as temporary bridge building. I recall being taken by my parents to see the results of this training which had been made available to the public. The quality of the work remains with me to this day, and I found the dug-outs and trenches extremely well made as well as the pontoon bridge over the river adjacent to the railway bridge which alas, is no longer there, being a victim of the Dr Beeching axe.

The town was given one of the first models of the Tank or Mobile fortress and I remember this being driven through the High street and turning down into Lion street en route for Bailey Park, where it stood for many years on the specially constructed plinth. It is no longer there, and I wonder what became of it.

For about a hundred years, the railway featured largely in the fortunes of the Borough, as it became the principle means of employment requiring many trades and crafts. The former London and North Western Railway made it a centre for its operations in the area, and the District Operating Superintendent, as well as the district Civil Engineer and Locomotive Superintendent were located at Brecon Road. With the decline of the railway, these centres of operation have now long gone, and the building of the new link road between the river bridge carrying the Merthyr road and Brecon road has successfully covered what remained of the landmarks of the locomotive sheds and workshops. There is little to show that a railway line existed to Brynmawr and beyond except the remains of the bridge buttresses which now form an entrance to the lane leading to the cemetery.

And yet the area was busy and bustling with activity as much of this originated with the need to transfer coal from the adjacent pits at Blaenavon and the coal mining areas beyond to Dowlais and Merthyr to the North of England. Where stood the Signal Box controlling trains to Govilon and on, as well as to the running sheds and workshops, a new footbridge connecting Union Road to Nevill Hall Hospital marks the spot. Where R.A. McLennan's office was sited diagonally opposite, is now covered with a new footpath, and the remainder of the site has been levelled out, perhaps in preparation for the acceptance of some new style factories. Who can tell? The future would seem to favour the operation of small units rather than large.

The ghosts of all those most agreeable men come to life as I reminisce. Robert Manuel, John Beckwith, John Evenson, David Watts and so many more. Many of them served not only the railway but also the town, and John Beckwith, Albert Wytcherly, Jack Thurston and George Tranter all became Mayor of the Borough. That is when it *was* a borough.

A favourite walk of mine is along the river bank to Llanwenarth Church, thence along the lane from the church past Red Barn to the Brecon road. In former days it was alive with life, as sandmartins were abundant, nesting in the sandy banks of the river.

Llanwenarth Church. (A.S.H.)

Kingfishers were commonplace, roosting over quiet stretches of water waiting for the unwary minnow. The fields would be more colourful, with an abundance of buttercups, cowslips, meadowsweet, and red poppies. There does not seem to be any of this wildlife now, and bird life appears to be much less in evidence. Perhaps it is because I am no longer young and with failing sight and hearing, but I tend to think that it may well be to do with the use of fertilisers and insecticides. It does seem to be something of a paradox that the use of chemicals whilst undoubtedly increasing crop cultivation also works against the desire to restrict production to avoid the waste that this produces.

Ah well, it is all very difficult but I think that we have seen the best that this world has given to us so bountifully in past years. It may be downhill from here on, but the memories are very happy.

Cottage Hospital Hereford Road.

DICK HORSINGTON

Tiverton Place was the residential block for Tucker Brothers staff. It consisted of ten houses. Tucker Brothers were the first steam mill and bakery and they owned all the property from the Guildhall Public House to the Black Lion, and from the Coliseum to J.G. Thomas's yard.

The mill was built in two separate stages, first the flour mill and then the corn mill. It was driven by steam out of a boiler house at the rear. It had two steam boilers – coal fired – and a steam tube ran across Lion Street to the bakery. The boiler house was situated between the present Horsington's yard and the old Tuckers Mill building and would have discharged into the brick chimney between the boiler house and the machine room. Part of this chimney can be seen today in the brickwork built against the Town Wall. Continuing around the wall was the machine room for driving all machinery into the two parts of the mill.

Former Bush Inn

This later became Horsington Bros. stables. The shop on the corner of Lion Street was the retail outlet for Tucker Bros. The Coliseum was the site of their stables. Clams and the Shoe Cobblers was the residence of Tucker Brothers Bakers. Following these residences was Dover's the printers which was burnt out about 1910. Dover's moved to Frogmore Street. The Labour Party took over the building and later the Coliseum Company developed Jones the Cobblers, Garlands the Basket Shop and a residence. The present Horsington's Yard was the Blacksmiths shop and shoeing shop for Tuckers horses and the machinery maintenance.

Tucker Brothers went bankrupt in 1905 and the Mill was bought by Horsington Brothers in 1907 for £750.

Tuckers shop became Ruther's the greengrocers. They were followed by McFisheries and then Bradleys and so to Fosters. The Guildhall Public House was turned into a shop in 1914 when Trevor Scott moved out, and is now a Travel Agents. Next door is Digby Turners which was Phillips the shoe shop and before that the Home and Colonial.

Lewis's Iron Foundry site along with Dover's site were the 2nd Established Roman Catholic Church and Cloisters. Lewis, the ironfounder, was a journeyman craftsman from Merthyr. He was supported by Sir Benjamin Hall (Big Ben) of Llanover. He had castings made for the Government; Hyde Park railings, St Mary's Church railings at Usk and St Mary's Church railings at Abergavenny and the Old Cemetery gates were all out of the same casting pit.

The casting room is now the Wicker Workshop and Craft Centre in Lewis's Lane and has metal framework and battens in the roof.

The India and China Tea Company established the Liberal Club on the first floor of the Lewis's Lane building and this in due course became the residence of the Burton Bakery and grocery staff. The freehold of Lewis's Iron Foundry belonged to Mr Lane of Westgate House, Union Road, Abergavenny and he also owned the five residences in Lion Street which are now Lane's Garage. The India China Tea Company steam Bakery took over the Tuckers's Bakery side of the business and eventually became Burton's Bakery and then Alderton's Brothers Bakery. Part of the Bakery was the retail cake and food shop which is now Giles Windows. In the extreme corner was the entrance door to the weigh-bridge which was in the road off Lion Street. The bakery was finally sold to Harry's Carpets.

The old LNW railway bridge on Pen-y-pound with Toll House on right through arch. 1947

The grocer's shop was sold to Garfield Weston who sold out to Hippo Campo when he developed Fine Fare but he did not get the chance to buy the bakehouse.

The first floor of the bakehouse was divided offices, with the bull nosed window above the weigh-bridge cabin and known as the lighthouse. This was for many years the headquarters of the Women's Institute for Monmouthshire under the Presidency of Miss Martha Jackson of Chain Cottage, Chain Lane, Abergavenny.

The ten dwellings known as Tiverton Place survived the bankruptcy settlement and were eventually sold to William Horsington by Miss Tucker in 1930s. Later they were bought by the Town Council and demolished to make the present car park.

Following on from the Tiverton Place block of houses was the first Masonic Lodge which eventually became Jefferies seed stores, and is now a furniture store for Straker Chadwick's. The Tiverton Place sign is on this building. At one time about 1900 it was the Salvation Army Hall. Next door is now the John Sullivan warehouse. This used to be Williams the Vet, before he moved to Henton House. Now the D.H.S.S. in Monk Street. In front of Sullivan's warehouse were the residential offices of Tucker Bros. After their removal it became Percy Wibberley the Auctioneer who was followed by Montague Harris and whose successor moved to their present office.

Vine Tree

The Granville West and Morgan Offices in Central Chambers is a reasonably new building.

Knight's barbers shop was part of the Black Lion Public House.

The Farmers Arms has always been a Pub.

Diana's was Turners the grocers.

The cottage next door was owned by Mrs Humphry of Old Court and was lived in by a gardener.

Mrs Newman's sweet shop is now Rennie's the estate agents.

The Newmarket Inn was bulldozed down to make room for the entrance to the Brewery Yard Car park.

The group of six cottages are now Lane's Showrooms.

They were lived in by Oliver Smart an engineer; Offers a haycutter; Dickie Adams, cattle drover; Mrs and Miss MacLinden, two Irish ladies; George (Busty) Parsons, who was a sailor of the 1914/18 war who rescued the Tzar of Russia at the time of the Russian Revolution and was presented with a silver cigarette case for his services. He was Mrs Matthew-Hudsons brother-in-law.

Old St Johns Square where now stands the Post Office. Note the old Vine Tree archway into Chicken Street. About 1940.

Round the corner into Monk Street is Gabb's.

Across the road is Linden House originally owned by Dr Gamble then Dr Tresawna then Mrs Bennett (Miss Bunn) and so to the N.H. Depot.

The Cattle Market was a field and the Bethany Baptist Chapel was sited here before being moved and built by J.G. Thomas.

Mr Haig surveyor developed the original Cattle Market, the Slaughterhouse and Fire Station.

Beyond Market Lane was Robert Price's stone cutters yard and residence. There is the Kings head monogram on the wall at the end of King Street. This Robert Price was the great-great-grand-father of the present generation.

Cross the road to J.G. Thomas's yard and next were the wagon sheds of Tuckers Mill.

The Christadelphian Hall was the Welfare and Union Hall of Tuckers Staff.

The Tannery

The Tanners Arms, Tan House and Philpotts Mill with Gough's Skin Yard in Lower Monk Street, were the tanning and wool stapling group, with their drying ground on Caenata bank. The water for these tanneries was directly from the Gavenny. Also in Lower Monk Street were two Farriers – Amos Jones and William Parry with four other blacksmiths in the town.

Between the Tanners Arms and the Tunns Public House was the original Workhouse.

Tudor Street at that time stretched from the Tudor Arms – on the corner of Byfield Lane and ended at Nevill Hall on the Brecon Road. This was still part of Tudor Street until the new Workhouse was built and it became Union Road.

From Byfield Lane there was a ford to cross the river and walk to Llanfoist.

There was a swimming pool in the river which was situated at the nearest point that one could walk from the Castle. The charge was one penny.

Blacksmiths in the town were:

> Tuckers Mill,
>
> Davies Lion Works.
>
> Amos Jones, Lower Monk Street.
>
> William Parry, Lower Monk Street.
>
> Bill Symonds at Philpotts Mill.
>
> Charles Morgan, Lewis's Iron Foundry.

Post Second War clearance

The double fire forges at the Marquis of Abergavenny's Town House in the present Lower Castle Street. (Two suspended bellow's were still suspended from the ceiling on right of courtyard).

The Industrial Product of the Gavenny stream was power for seven mills, the last of which has just been closed. (Triley Mill). The others were Philpotts, Duggans, Wibberleys, Priory, Mardy Park, Evans and Fforest Coalpit.

The Terrible Flood of 8th May 1931 washed through the course of the Gavenny from Fforest Coalpit to Philpotts Mill. It reached 6 feet in depth on the Monmouth Road opposite Miss Black's Garage and the houses of Lower Monk Street – Asylum Terrace and Mill street were flooded demolishing No. 1 Asylum Terrace. One lady drowned in Mill Street when the policeman trying to save her lost his grip. A taxi driver and two ladies spent hours on top of a bill posting board next door to the Bridge Inn before being rescued. As the flood rushed trough Swan Meadows it also carried away the Mill Street bridge.

The Cibi Brook. This stream was manually split at the back of the Herefordshire House Public House and one course ran through J.G. Thomas's Yard and through the car park between the Bethany Chapel and the Brewery. The other course ran immediately at the back of Frogmore Street properties, through Cibi Lane to pass under Harry's Carpets (originally the bakehouse) underground through the car park (formerly Tiverton Place) beside the Greyhound Bowling Green, then under Straker Chadwick's to reappear on the south side of the Brewery Car Park to join the other course. Together they proceeded under Laburnam House in Monk Street, under the Goal and The Rising Sun which is now the Coach and Horses. Under Cross Street and into Mill Street and so into the Mill pond of Duggans Mill, eventually reaching the Mill which has now gone, and so back into the Gavenny at the back of Coffin House which used to be at the back of the Abergavenny Hotel.

The Cibi was divided to ease the flow of the bulk water through the flat area of ground to prevent flooding. In the early part of the century the area before Queen Street would be flooded in the winter.

Winters were obviously much colder than now as skaters would skate on the frozen water and the energetic ones could skate on the Usk above the river bridge and it was possible to skate from Llanfoist to

Newport on the Canal in half an hour.

Philpotts Mill which was situated near to the Flowerland Nurseries on Monmouth Road was the home of the first aircraft variable pitch propeller invented by Walter Jones. He was the brother of Doug Jones who lived in Western Road for many years. The propeller was made in a shed at the rear of the Mill and was eventually sold to the Americans. Walter was also the inventor of a predecessor of the Hovercraft. He used a punt and fitted a motor car engine and a propeller above the engine to power the craft. This was in about 1919 whilst he was working for the Will's tobacco family.

Another intelligent and inventive man was Jack Phillips of Longtown and residing in 39 Monk Street (on the corner of Ross Road and Monk Street) now 6 Lower Monk Street. He invented a machine to wrap the salt for the Abergavenny Crisp Company. The blue paper twists.

He was also an exceptional radio pioneer. Others interested in this field were Douglas Singer, a school teacher, the Reverend D.D. Davies – curate of St Mary's, Ernie Jefferies – Corn Stores, Bert Norton a radio engineer and Charlie Howard a motor engineer.

The Mill

Whilst mentioning the field of radio it must be acknowledged that A.D. Russell-Clarke of Pen-Bidwal Lane, Pandy was a government adviser on Radio and Communication including Morse Code throughout the 1914/18 war.

Duggan the miller, Davies the iron founders and Oliver Smart devised a scheme to attach an electric generator to the Duggans Mill water wheel to electrify Mill Street and Cross Street but the commissioners at that time rejected the project.

Lower Castle Street was originally on the opposite side of the Angel. the proof being a stone window in the cellar of No. 14 Sydney George's bottom shop. It was removed and presented to the Abergavenny Museum by Messrs. Briggs (Sydney George). The street level of Cross Street at this point was obviously eight feet lower than at present (cellar floor level of Sydney George and the Angel). Sydney George's was built on the original Lower Castle Street with the first Catholic Church built in the rear.

It became Hansard's "Pop" Factory and Alfred Jackson's warehouse before it collapsed.

The Gunter Mansion was originally a gaol and prison for prisoners of the Franco-British War. It was a house with a thatched roof.

Taken down by Thomas Foster and in the course of the work a beautiful duelling sword was found among the roof timbers. A tombstone from Gunter House can be seen in the approach to the R.H. entrance to St Mary's Church.

Prior's Well. The Holy Well rises in front of the bungalow in Holywell Road and feeds the drinking trough. This was the first drinking supply to the Priory. They collected water in a bucket and had to carry it over the river to the Priory.

PHILIP LOVELL[*]

I'm glad to have lived in Abergavenny and to have known it in the early part of the twentieth century. I don't think I'd like to be starting life now in spite of the advantages of this modern age and the supposed improvement in the quality of life.

That is the feeling that comes out of the reminiscences of a number of Abergavenny's older citizens recalled to the Abergavenny and District Civic Society for the purpose of compiling this book. But it is another indication of the British propensity for remembering more the good things of life and almost completely locking away the hardships and struggles.

Most of us who recall the experiences of the last

---

[*] Phillip Lovell started compiling the original book some years ago, but then fell ill and was unable to continue. His contribution is published in tribute to this work, but readers should bear in mind that they will find some passages also occur in the texts by some of the other writers.

war, for instance, are more keen to describe the comradeship, the sharing, the sacrifices and good deeds of others, the joy of little things like home-made entertainment in the shelters while bombs were blowing our homes to bits. The real delight of Molly Cox's blacked-out fish and chip shop where in the heady atmosphere and hazy smoke of the fryer you chatted amiably with your neighbour as you waited for what you still remember as the best chips in the county, the Forces' dances at the Swan Hotel, and the sunrise over the Little Skirrid to thankfully welcome another day.

And it is the little things of pleasure that this book records as its contributors look back. They draw a colourful picture of an Abergavenny which took pride in its history and its tradition, its treasures, its progress, its people and its contribution to the life of Wales and the world.

In their days our predecessors will have looked back perhaps with similar longing to an even more Spartan and seemingly more enjoyable times, and in fifty years time those who survive the present period in the history of the town – a period which has perhaps experienced the greatest changes – will no doubt be saying too "I'm glad I lived when I did" . . . such is human nature.

As we grow older we often think we can remember events of fifty, sixty or seventy years ago more clearly than those of more recent years. But the memory plays tricks and often one person's recollections do not tally with those of another. Nevertheless the general picture of life in Abergavenny of yesteryear comes through clearly and is worth recording for posterity because what comes out most clearly is how much of Abergavenny has gone, not only in bricks and mortar, in trees and fields and landscape, but in activity and customs and way of life.

Most contributors remembered Abergavenny as a railway town. Not only was the railway the principal source of employment with the great locomotive depot in Brecon Road and the three busy stations which served passenger and freight traffic from far and wide, but the built-up area of the town was largely confined by the railway line as it swept across the Usk and round in a big arc to the foot of the Little Skirrid. Beyond the line were the rural lower slopes of the Sugar Loaf and the Deri and the village of Mardy.

That sweeping line with its embankments and its

bridges across the Usk and across Brecon Road and Pen-y-Pound has now gone but the memory of the journey from Abergavenny up through the Clydach Gorge and over the mountain to Tredegar and Merthyr is ever green and frequently described.

The carriages themselves were gorgeous. They were in rich maroon with gold lining and with outward opening doors which seemed to be set back into the doorway and shiny brass handrails and handles. They were open type so that you could walk between the seats, and the luggage racks were up over each seat, again in brass and the whole thing very ornately done.

It was unfortunate that when the line was transferred from the Midland Region to the Western Region of British Rail it was discovered that these carriages were out of gauge and so they were sent to Caerphilly where they were burned. In their place were provided auto-cars, the push-pull variety with the door in the centre, and this gave rise to problems at stations like Clydach where the platform curves sharply. With a door at each end of the carriage passengers could step down easily, but with a door in the centre there was a gap of twelve to eighteen inches between the carriage and the platform, and so a board had to be provided to bridge it.

Travelling the line when the autumn mists were about was magic. We would leave Brecon Road station with a shrill little whistle, go down past the loco sheds and give another whistle, across the bridge over the Usk, through the cutting at Llanfoist, round by the old Llanfoist brewery and on to the steepest part of the line between Llanfoist and Gilwern, gaining height in the easier countryside ready for the haul through Clydach Gorge itself.

Others remember the thrill of shorter, but equally enjoyable journeys – to Llanfoist or Govilon for a picnic by the canal, to the Junction station for a walk up the Holy Mountain or to Monmouth Road station to climb the Little Skirrid or even all the way to Nantyderry to pick wild flowers in the woods.

In those days of steam Abergavenny was full of the sounds of the railway and nothing was more emphatic than the shrill whistle and frantic puffing of the banking engines which helped to haul long trains up the gradient from Monmouth Road station to the Junction and on to Llanvihangel.

"We used to rush to the bridge (on the Old Monmouth Road) to watch them go under and be enveloped in the steam of two and sometimes three engines".

There were long trains, too, coming down the Merthyr line, especially when excursions were run to faraway places.

These trains were worked up the various branch lines from Cardiff, Caerphilly, Bargoed, Merthyr, Dowlais, Nine Mile Point, Ebbw Vale and Abersychan to be brought together at Brynmawr before going down the bank to Abergavenny and then to Hereford and beyond.

One such trip in February, 1937 was a Thursday (early closing day) excursion to Birmingham, to see a choice of three pantomimes, or on to Coventry. The return fare from Abergavenny was 4s.6d. (22½p) to Birmingham and 6s.0d. (30p) to Coventry, leaving Abergavenny at 1.55 pm. arriving in the wee small hours.

There were excursions to Abergavenny, too, on special occasions and one such was the Abergavenny and Border Counties show, then held in Bailey Park. Special trains were run for the conveyance of livestock as well as passengers and the railway company had its own office on the show ground with information of trains, etc.

Extra trains were run for market days, and special trains for annual outings now recalled with much pleasure, and most look back with sadness at the closure of the depot and the running of the last train to and from Merthyr in January, 1958.

Castle Lane

Many were the excursions which came to Abergavenny and most memorable were those of the Whitsun marches when people from churches in the valleys came in their hundreds by special trains to Merthyr Road and then walked with banners and bands, singing and holding hands, through the town to Abergavenny Castle for a great rally and great junketing.

Everyone was in his or her Sunday best (something unknown in recent days) and there was real excitement and joy in parading and in renewing acquaintanceships. Many a romance blossomed on the Whitsun march and couples still say, with happy memories, "We first met at Abergavenny Castle."

There were, too, regular school and club outings which included dinners and teas served at the Castle by the resident caterers. Sometimes there were as many as two thousand mouths to feed and on the day of the Investiture of Prince Edward as the Prince of Wales, which was a national holiday, no fewer than 4,288 people were catered for in three huge marquees and the dining hall of the Castle Keep.

On Summer Bank Holidays these parties invariably finished up with huge firework displays before people made their way back to Brecon Road station for the journey home. The coming of the motor car saw the end of this tradition.

As Abergavenny was a market town, the railway and Brecon Road station in particular was much used for the conveyance of livestock and many have recalled how sheep and cattle were driven on the hoof from the Market through Lion Street, Frogmore Street and Brecon Road when the town was thronged with market day shoppers.

And it was the railway (Great Western) which provided one of the first bus services in the area.

High Street Pedestrianised. (R.M.J.)

Frogmore Street, entrance to Precinct. (P.N.H.)

Precinct. (P.N.H.)

Precinct. (P.N.H.)

This was introduced in about 1906 and ran from Abergavenny to Brecon once a day, using a double-decker bus driven by a Milne Daimler petrol engine. Before that the route to Crickhowell and Brecon was served by a horse-drawn wagon operated by Evans the carrier, a journey described as "thrilling" by someone who was then seven years old.

Thrilling may well have been only one of the adjectives used to describe the outings provided by the solid tyre open brakes which were used by the GWR for

72

excursions for its own and other firms' employees. Carrying as many as forty straw-hatted or bonnetted passengers at a time, the great monsters would take the dusty country roads to some favoured beauty spot or hostelry for a day or afternoon out, and wise was the passenger who thought to bring a cushion.

Abergavenny then, perhaps even more than now, had its share of local beauty spots and places for an enjoyable outing or picnic – St Mary's Vale, the Sugar Loaf, the Blorenge, the Skirrids, the canal and the riverside.

Monmouth road station 1992. (P.N.H.)

Great Western Hotel. (P.N.H.)

A favourite walk was along the river bank from the Usk bridge at Llanfoist to Llanwenarth Church and back along the lane to the Red Barn and Brecon Road.

And what a delight it was to climb the Little Skirrid, the smallest of the seven hills of Abergavenny. There was a well halfway up where we always stopped for a drink of water. We would carry on up through the wood and to us youngsters it was just like exploring the unknown land of North America. Occasionally we would come to a clearing and have a view of part of the

74

town below, and then it was on into the undergrowth again to make our way to the top.

There at the summit was a flagpole and on high days and holidays a flag would be flown, reminding people of the town of their heritage and making us proud that we lived in such a place. Looking down we were near enough to the town to pick out familiar landmarks – the street where we lived and perhaps even the house and the window of the bedroom.

Leading into the woods at the foot of the Skirrid was what was then called the Rope Walk, a lovers' lane of very happy memories which led from Lower Monk Street across the Gavenny, up Firs Lane and over the railway footbridge. It was a regular walk for courting couples – a pleasure curtailed by the building of the Eastern by-pass.

Industry and employment in Abergavenny has changed considerably over the years. Long gone are many of the traditional activities and crafts and redevelopment has left only traces of the mills and factories, workshops and establishments which made the town largely self-supporting. Gone too are the sounds and smells and those familiar sights which often marked the time of day or week and spelled security and contentment.

Horsedrawn vehicles were the means of transport for the tradesman as well as the traveller and the regular deliveries by the baker and milkman, brewer and carrier were all part of a life that was orderly and predictable.

Burtons, the bakers, for instance, stabled their horses in Lewis's Lane and every morning they would be led in a long train down the lane and across Frogmore Street into Lion Street where the bakery – had ready the delivery vans already loaded with sweet-smelling bread and confectionery.

Earlier this bakery was owned and managed by Tucker Brothers, who had established the town's first steam mill on the other side of the road. The mill was built in two separate stages, first the flour mill and then the corn mill, and they were driven by steam from the coal-fired boiler house in the rear where there were two boilers and from where steam was piped across Lion Street to the bakery.

At the turn of the century Tucker Brothers owned all the property from the Guildhall public house at the beginning of Frogmore Street to the Black Lion Inn at the corner of Market Street and from the Coliseum to the corner of King Street, including Tiverton Place which was made up of ten houses for Tucker's staff.

The shop on the corner of Lion Street (now Fosters) was the retail outlet. The Coliseum cinema now stands on the site of the original stables and the two shops next door – were the Tuckers' residence. Horsington's Yard was the blacksmith's shop for shoeing and machinery maintenance.

Tucker Brothers went bankrupt in 1905 and Horsington Brothers bought the mill in 1907 for £750. The corner shop became Ruthers the greengrocers, and was subsequently occupied by McFisheries, Bradleys and then Fosters.

Nevill Hall hospital. (R.M.J.)

The bakery was owned in turn by the India and China Tea Company, Burtons and then Alderton Brothers, with the retail shop in that part now occupied by Giles Windows and the end portion containing the weighbridge. The floor above, with its bullnose window known as the Lighthouse, was converted to offices and for many years was the headquarters of the Monmouthshire Federation of Women's Institute whose president then was Mrs Martha Jackson, of Chain Cottage, Chain Lane.

Opposite in Tiverton Place was the town's first Masonic Lodge which eventually became Jefferies' seed store and now rebuilt as an auction room for Straker, Son and Chadwick. At one time – in about 1900 – it was the Salvation Army Hall. The warehouse next door, in recent days used by Vin Sullivan, was the premises of Mr Williams, the veterinary surgeon, before he moved to Monk Street.

The wagon shed of Tucker's Mill were on the corner of King Street in what became J.G. Thomas's yard, and the next door Christadelphian Hall was originally the Welfare and Union Hall of Tucker's staff.

These have now gone, as also has the Newmarket Inn, further east along Lion Street, which was demolished to make room for the entrance to the Brewery Yard car park.

Lane's car showrooms next door were a group of six cottages lived in by Oliver Smart, an engineer, Mr Offer, a hay cutter, Dickie Adams, a cattle drover, two Irish ladies, Mrs and Miss MacLinden, and George (Busty) Parsons, who was a sailor in the 1914-18 War and one of the party who rescued the Tzar of Russia at the time of the Russian Revolution. He proudly owned an inscribed silver cigarette case presented to him for his part in the operation.

Returning to Lewis's Lane, here was Lewis's iron foundry alongside Dover's printing works which earlier had been the town's Roman Catholic Church and cloisters. Lewis, the iron founder, was a journeyman craftsman from Merthyr. He was supported by Sir Benjamin Hall (Big Ben) of Llanover who had castings made for the Government as well as Hyde Park railings and the railings of St Mary's Church, Usk; and St Mary's Priory Church at Abergavenny and the cemetery gates in Old Hereford Road were all out of the same casting pit. What was the casting pit is now the site of the wicker work shop and craft centre, Stables, which has a metal framework and metal battens in the roof.

Prominent among other industry at the beginning of the century and still very much in living memory was Seargeant Bros' printing works and paper bag factory in Queen Street.

Here was a large workforce of women who made paper bags of every description which were supplied to establishments throughout Wales and across the border, while the printing works turned out a high standard of letterpress as well as impeccable binding, carrying the imprint of Seargeants and Abergavenny far and wide.

A well-remembered feature of the establishment was the hooter which daily called employees to work and provided an accurate time check for the rest of the town, something which was missed during the war years when it was silenced to prevent confusion with the air raid warning.

Seargeants occupied much of the area now taken up by the Cibi Walk shopping precinct.

RICHARD MERTON-JONES

My earliest memories are of living in Avenue Road at a house called The White Cottage opposite the cricket field (and now occupied by Mr and Mrs William Farley. My parents built this house in 1921 – the year I was born – and my two brothers and I were looked after by Alice Nash, her first job after leaving school, and she is an elder sister of Ted Nash, a distinguished citizen of the town and President of the Abergavenny Cricket Club. Alice afterwards achieved distinction as a Nanny with some very important families and is now living in Abergavenny in retirement.

One of my most vivid early memories was the day Woolworths opened (probably 1924 or 25). I remember the building being altered from Butts, a man's clothes shop which moved down to Cross Street into what is now the Dorothy Café – and the day Woolworths opened, everyone was presented with a free bucket – but one had to battle for it and I well remember being taken along (with my two brothers) by Alice to collect our bucket – and feeling a very small chap amongst an enormous, heaving mass of grown-ups!

Above Cross Street, view of upper stories. *Below* The Great George 1992. (P.N.H.)

It may be appropriate here to recall some of the old shops and buildings which have disappeared. On the corner of High Street and Market Street, the present Furnells Radio Shop was Pipers Penny Bazaar where we bought small toys in a long narrow shop with toys on both sides. Next door to this was an interesting hardware shop displaying large earthenware bowls, baskets, etc. hung externally and this was kept by a man who caused rather a local scandal when discovered syphoning petrol from people's cars. A little further along High Street was the Greyhound Hotel (now Times Furnishing and Olivers) and this was a most interesting old coaching inn with central wide entrance going straight through to the stable yard at the rear (Market Street). The loss of this most interesting old hostelry was part of a great reduction in the number of public houses – one of the most significant being the large building at the corner of Monk Street and Lower Monk Street (being next to the Pavilion Cinema and now used as flats), which was the London Hotel. And another, nearby, was the Newmarket Inn in Lion Street – part of which is now Rennie's Office but the bulk demolished and now part of car park.

At the top of Cross Street in the building recently

rebuilt for Boots – was a large, high class ladies' dress shop (where my father always felt that my mother spent all his money!) kept by a Mr and Mrs Trevor Jones (who had two pretty daughters, one of whom at nineteen married Dr Davies who was thirty-one! and the other married Curtis-Sanders of Santon, Newport – and a son Val – but all have left the area) - who shocked the town by going bankrupt, and then restarting opposite just below the King's Head in what was the Golden Fleece but is now a Chinese Restaurant. In Market Street was Facey's Brewery (opposite Chadwicks' Office) and – nearby – the Fire Station was in Lion Street in part of the Cattle Market facing Market Street – both solid stone buildings of character. There was also a much larger brewery at Llanfoist – which I often walked past after we moved out to Llanfoist in 1929, but the site of which has been redeveloped with houses.

Before we moved to Llanfoist, I had, of course, started school and this was in a small school in the old Priory adjoining St Mary's Church – this being a beautiful building, a wonderful feature adding greatly to the scene and the approach to the town on Monmouth Road, buy sadly demolished just after the last war.

At this small school, we had as a pupil, Francis Pym (recent Foreign Secretary) who was the son of Leslie Pym an Estate Agent who later became our M.P., following Captain Jack Herbert (father of Mr Robin Herbert) who had followed Sir Leolin Forestier-Walker. My father took us to school in the family car, a 1925 bull-nosed Morris Cowley which, during the winter, required water draining and refilling every night and morning, but was difficult to start and caused our being late for school frequently.

In these early days, my father, after war service, took pride in the Town's War Memorial designed by Gilbert Ledward who my father had recommended as being a suitable person for the commission. We used to get invited to military displays in Bailey Park and, most years, there would be a large Territorial Army camp in the Castle Meadows, with units from other parts of the Country. I remember the start of the Red and White Bus Company, with one or two small buses which regularly broke down and, while they grew, smaller companies prospered – Griffin from Brynmawr (later part of Red and White) and Morgans, Govilon, a small private concern with taxis, hearse, etc, but now defunct. But it was really as a railway centre that Abergavenny was known. We had three busy railway stations – Great Western (now Monmouth Road), Junction, (now closed) where branch lines joined) and Brecon Road (now demolished) where the branch line from "the Valleys" (Brynmawr, etc.) arrived. There were also the large "Engine Sheds" in Union Road to which we used to be taken by Alice Nash's father (an engine driver) to see and board the engines on a Sunday morning.

I remember the General Strike of 1926 – and standing outside Barclays Bank while huge crowds thronged and a large parade of strikers with bands etc., marched through the town. In the 1930s traffic was two-way right through the town and on crowded market and summer days, monumental traffic jams arose. Imagine two buses or heavy lorries meeting outside the recently demolished Fine Fare (then a large butchers shop, D.E. Williams). The Coliseum Cinema was an old establishment but the Pavilion was a "rush job" contrived by the Coliseum owners. We had heard rumours of an Odeon coming to the town. From then on through the war – we were well served with two cinemas each showing two films a week (or one for the whole week if exceptionally good). We had the Angel Hotel – much as it is now – where the best dances and parties were held.

After we moved to Llanfoist in 1929 one of our main areas of recreation was the canal – both walking and rowing. Periodically our lives would be affected by the River Usk flooding – the Castle Meadows being entirely under water and the main road to town blocked by the old gas works. In May 1931 we had a terrible night of thunder rain when much of old Mill Street was washed away and a woman was drowned. A house adjoining the Gavenny in Lower Monk Street was demolished and has never been rebuilt. The high water marks from that night remained painted on one of the road frontage motor showrooms in Monmouth Road (now demolished) and also on the steel columns of the old railway bridge over the Usk at Llanfoist (also demolished but replaced with the gas pipe eye-sore). When the road flooded here, we were occasionally allowed to walk home to Llanfoist over the railway bridge – which was much higher and never flooded – but mostly we could only get home by taking a train to Govilon (where there was a station) and walking back to Llanfoist (where there was not).

When I left school, shortly before the war, I joined my father in his architects' practice in Monk Street and our short cut to work was through the then fully built-up, narrow, twisty Tudor Street and Castle Street – and down Lower Castle Street (Angel Lane) where there was no one-way system.

Post Office 1992. (R.M.J.)

Health Centre, Tudor Street. (R.M.J.)

Department of Employment. (R.M.J.)

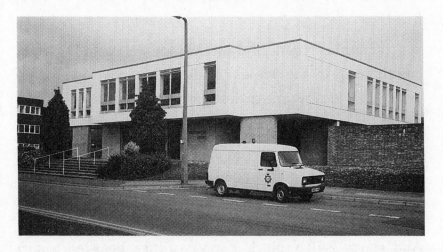

Police Station and Magistrates' Court. (R.M.J.)

I remember electricity coming to Abergavenny, in 1935. For months beforehand we had watched the steel pylons being erected over the Skirrid (there was no Civic Society or planning controls in those days), and getting nearer and nearer to the switch-on by the Mayor, a Councillor Tillman, I believe. I remember various Mayors – some of whom had the job more than once – contrasted by the stately, dignified Colonel Bishop and the flamboyant Max Beveridge – a short, fat, jolly man who kept a drapery shop in Brecon Road. During the war he did a voluntary job as a Welfare Officer which allowed him to dispense petrol coupons to soldiers on leave – so that we had to keep in with him!

I remember years of agitation for a swimming pool culminating in the present Bailey Park pool opened in 1936. This is now much less prized than it was in our youth.

Abergavenny has always had its share of characters – I remember, a rag and bone man in White Horse Lane (soon to be linked to our glamorous new shopping precinct!) mostly drunk and trouble with the police. And Harry Wilks (black Harry) a filthy, bearded tramp in bowler hat, etc. We had many more distinguished characters – a few of whom survive to this day – but we no longer see the City Fathers assembling nightly in the corner of the Angel Bar to settle the affairs of the world. I recall Robert Godfrey (Raif's father), George Goodwin (head of the Lion Engineering Works – trousers at half mast and size 14 boots), Max Beveridge (previously mentioned) and George (Hookie) Walker (Manager of Ebbw Vale Labour Exchange). A mixed assortment!

We have had our share of notoriety. There was a national scandal when a local Solicitor disappeared leaving large debts – and he was later located in the Foreign Legion. Later – during the war – there was a nationally publicized homosexual scandal resulting in instant dismissal of the then cinema manager.

Abergavenny has always had strong sporting action. The rugby side has always done well and I remember long-serving full back, Reuben Price, and I was in Bailey Park the day Ivor Cook had his skull fractured with a noise like a gun crack. Soccer-wise the Abergavenny Thursdays did well to get to First Division of Welsh League (Vin Sullivan was one of the keen men) – and this spilled over to Llanfoist where in the 1930s there was a strong side including one Bob Webb who is still about at a great age! I used to play hockey where the town was always strong and produced many international players – but I was not one of them!

Medieval buildings restored. (P.N.H.)

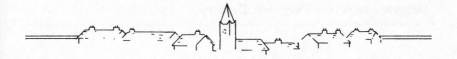

CHARLES PRICE

I was born on the 21st December 1909 at No. 2 Trinity Terrace, Baker Street, Abergavenny.

One of my earliest memories as a small boy of five was watching the Battalion of the 3rd Mon Regiment assembling on the area between the old Drill Hall and the old Police Station before being marched off to the First World War. It was a wonderful sight with all these men marching, headed by their band, down Baker Street and right through the centre of the town up to the Great Western Station.

I also remember the very strict food rationing we had during the war with very little eggs, meat or butter.

In 1915 my family moved to 15 Nevill Street where my grandfather had started the firm of C. Price and Son, painters and decorators, in 1885. Therefore, from a very early age I lived and worked in Nevill Street until I retired in 1973.

The family lived in No. 15 until we moved to a new house in Chapel Road in 1932. I will always have very fond memories of Nevill Street with its wealth of fifteenth, sixteenth and seventeenth century buildings and also for all the streets in the centre of Abergavenny surrounded by the remains of the old Town Wall. Perhaps it would be best to discuss some of the old houses in Nevill Street and St John's Square and mention some of the characters living in this street.

No. 1 Nevill Street has been occupied by chemists continually from 1835, but previous to this date No. 1 and No. 3, now occupied by Bill Evans, estate agent, was an hotel called The Raven. No. 3 was occupied by Mr H.P. Cadle, grocer and for many years a councillor until he lost his seat, much to his great annoyance. No. 2, opposite the chemist, was Mr Price the tailor, a very portly gentleman with white hair who always seemed to me to be standing on the top of the three steps leading into his shop. His daughter, Marylin Thomas, became a well-known actress and recently figured in the Press at a farewell party given to her by Sir Peter Hall. She was then ninety-two. Montague Burton's premises prior to 1915 was the Westwood Garage. For many years No. 5 Nevill Street was occupied by Mr and Mrs

Beverly Burton until they moved to No. 11 Nevill Street, a very fine seventeenth century house. According to the 1951 Census there were three private schools in Nevill Street at Nos. 19 and 23. No. 13 was known as Nidra House, has again become a school. In 1915 approximately it was occupied by a French lady, Madam Ardin. Perhaps she thought No. 13 was an unlucky number so she reversed her name and called it Nidra House.

She opened a draper shop next door to the tailor and it was there as a business for many years.

There are a few outstanding examples of fifteenth and sixteenth century buildings such as No. 14, the Cow Inn, No. 21 and the Kings Arms, all three circa 1550, and possibly No. 14, according to the Department of Ancient Buildings, Aberystwyth, might possibly be fourteenth century. The original occupiers were probably the Vaughan family as on the oak sill of one of the first floor windows is the coat of arms of the Vaughan family.

No. 21. The front elevation of this house was a magnificent oak framed structure with seven carved and fluted oak posts supporting the upper part of the building. The posts have all disappeared and have been replaced by four cast iron posts and the whole of the original wattle and daub plaster panelling and oak framing have been covered with four inch thick mortar.

The Kings Arms has some of the original oak partition wall of 1550.

For many years Nevill Street was called Rother Street which the Oxford Dictionary describes as an Anglo Saxon word for horned cattle. Rother street was used as a cattle market. Farmers brought in their stock the day, or a few days, before and kept them in the Castle Meadows to recover after their long trip to the town, hence the two public houses, The Bull, on the present site of the Post Office, and The Cow, No. 14.

 Of course, there were many interesting houses and buildings in Tudor Street and Castle Street.

One of them was J. Irving who lived at No. 19 Nevill Street. He and his brother Edwin came from Dolgellau and set up a printing press known as the Minerva Press. John Irving was extremely well known throughout Wales especially for conducting *eisteddfodau*, not only national *eisteddfodau* but also in all the small villages and chapels throughout South Wales. Due to his great popularity he had many visitors and I remember well one outstanding visitor who came quite a number of times. He was Captain Geoffrey Crawshay, of Llanfair Court, and ex-Guards officer, very tall and very handsome and always dressed in a most distinctive manner. He also was a great Welshman, a great supporter of the Liberal Party and founder of the famous Captain Geoffrey Crawshay Rugby XV which consisted mainly of players of inter-national reputation.

No. 14, Nevill Street. (A.S.H.)

John Owen, in addition to his great love of *eisteddfodau*, had two other passions, one was driving motorcycles and then later small cars. In approximately 1922 he had a motorcycle and sidecar combination and invited my brother and me for a ride in his sidecar. He took us along the Brecon road towards Crickhowell and at one stage he told us "Look boys. We're doing nearly thirty-two miles an hour" and took both his hands right and left off the steering and said "God, isn't this wonderful!" Perhaps he didn't say God as he was a very religious man. His other great love was astronomy and he often asked us to come and have a look through his telescope at the moon or the stars, especially on a clear starry night. He had a very large telescope on a tripod stand and he would stand this on a raised platform at the end of his garden. John was also very fond of conjuring tricks. When he had learnt a new trick he left his office to demonstrate his skill to all his friends in Nevill Street, starting with Mr Fred Rose the jeweller, then to Mr Harry Cadle and lastly to Mr Sammy Tuck.

Next door to John Owen at No. 17 was a shop selling secondhand clothes which was also a registry for domestic servants. Now it is a cycle shop. This shop was addition to having only one leg had a rather terrifying appearance and to us small boys appeared to be a bit of a witch. I'm afraid she was anything but friendly and of small boys she had a particular dislike and was never too pleased for us to be near her shop door. Every Saturday, being the Jewish Sabbath, the shop remained closed. On one occasion on a Saturday a young couple were looking at her window and laughing and talking. I saw the old lady at one of the upstairs windows and she asked them to go away. They took no notice and a few moments later she came to the window again carrying what appeared to be like a bedroom vessel. A moment later a stream of water poured down on the unlucky couple.

I always had a very pleasant memory of the bakery at the rear of No. 14 Nevill Street which in 1914 was occupied by Mr Higgins, baker. The exotic smell of baking bread and cakes was irresistible to small boys especially when a doughnut was taken out of the oven too hot to hold was given to us. And talking of food reminds me of Mr and Mrs Harding's faggot and green pea shop in Flannel Street. This was our standard lunch on every Saturday and they were excellent. Mr Harding was a postman and Mrs Harding was responsible for making the faggots and an excellent job she made of making the faggots and an excellent job she made of them.

Another well-known postman of the town was Mr Thomas, a most cheerful and happy man who also kept a small grocers shop at the corner of St John's Street and Tudor Street.

St John's Lane.

Under the arches leading from St John Street to St John's Square lived the notorious or famous Denny Taylor. Den was a very short, but very strong man, rather fond of beer. He was a second-hand clothes and rag and bone merchant and lived with his mother in a small cottage in St John's Square.

As soon as he came back to Abergavenny from one of his frequent visits away, he immediately paid up any of his outstanding debts. I remember him coming to me on more than one occasion to pay me a few shillings for a little scrap iron which he had bought previous to one of his spells in prison. When Den was well and truly "oiled" he would conduct his own auction. First of all he would put his little cart up in the square and then from the depths of his cottage he would bring out everything, old pictures, framed or otherwise, bottles, clothing and an immense variety of goods. Then Den would stand on the cart, a small crowd would gather and the auction began. Any glass or pictures he could not sell he threw on the ground and jumped from his cart on to them. One day I was walking in Cross Street when I saw Den standing upright in his cart lashing the terrified pony into a wild gallop. He was as drunk as a lord, but he kept his balance as steady as a rock. His mad race down Cross Street reminded me of the chariot race in "Ben Hur". I'm sure he would not have disgraced himself in any Roman chariot race. The ale that was produced in the 1920s I'm sure was a much stronger brew than today's beer. Most weekends a fight would break out in St John's Square or Tudor Street and at holiday weekends it was a dead cert there would be more than one. It was mostly between men, but on rare occasions it was the women who were the attackers.

On one holiday weekend when the town was full of miners and steel men, tremendous commotions were going on in St John's Square. My bedroom was on the top floor of No. 16, but the row woke me up and I could see that the square and the bottom end of Nevill Street was teeming with people. Apparently the licensee of The Bull had kicked out one of the miners and caused him some serious injury to his eye. Consequently all the miners in other pubs came along for revenge on the licensee, Mr Edwards. I have a vivid memory of that night with hundreds of men yelling "Crucify him, crucify him," Edwards had taken care to barricade his door and windows. Those were the days!

In the 1920s I acquired a crystal set. It was always important to have the aerial as high as possible. I always wanted the best. Why not fix it on the tower of St John's Church? I had to apply to the masonic lodge who to my surprise gave me permission, so I had the thrill of climbing up a vertical ladder inside the tower to get out on to the roof. A further bonus was to hear the famous Russian bass Challiapin sing the Song of the Volga Boatmen and The Song of the Flea, on my crystal set. This was in 1924. Challiapin received the magnificent sum of £1500 from the BBC for three performances.

Tudor Street had many characters in the 1920s. Many will remember Joe Corrini, the Italian, who in the summer toured the town with his ice cream barrow and in the winter with his mobile organ with tunes from Italian operas. I always remember that he visited Pen-y-fal Road opposite the grammar school when I was there as a boy to play every Friday morning which gladdened the heart of most of us to realise there were only a few more hours of school for that week.

Then there was a Mr Griffiths, a genuine Gypsy who lived in a large three-storey house on the corner of Byfield Lane and Tudor Street, who went around the town with his horse and cart selling huge blocks of salt, eighteen inches to twenty-four inches long by approximately eight inches by eight inches.

Also I must not forget the little lady selling cockles from a little box on wheels once a week. She had already cooked the cockles by boiling them before selling them. And I must not forget Geoff Morgan of The Cross Keys Inn on the corner of Baker Street and Tudor Street. He was a very good rugby player who turned out for Newport and I think was also a trial player for the Welsh XV. His bar was festooned with pictures of famous boxers such as Jimmy Wild, Bombardier Wells, Gentleman Jim and many others. I was fascinated. A Mr and Mrs Winter and family ran the pub called The Bluebell in Tudor Street. This pub possessed outside a skittle alley at the rear of the house. The skittle balls were rolled back to base by means of stone slabs with a wide groove fixed in them atop a low wall. Several members of the Winter family still survive in Abergavenny. I remember that in Tudor Street there were three courts, A, B and C. Each court contained about four cottages open off Tudor Street. Sanitary arrangements were very basic.

At the bottom of Nevill Street and off Castle Street stands Old Court which was locally called Baker's Bailey. This house was for many generations the residence of the Baker family. The Bakers were stewards to the Lord of Abergavenny which passed to the Gabbs by marriage.

The only pub in Castle Street was The Old Duke. This was demolished some years ago. It was a great pity to see this rather interesting old pub go. It was a great rendezvous for men every Saturday at 12 noon. Opposite the Old Duke, but only for a very short while, we had a Chinese laundry. I remember it quite well. The owner had an English wife, but I'm afraid he was more of a curiosity than a viable laundryman. I can remember all the shops and businesses in Flannel Street and St John's Street, but no one stands out as an unusual character.

I think I ought to mention Market Day, Tuesday. In the 1920s there were very few cars, so farmers and their wives came in by horse and trap. There were also many privately run buses which operated on all the roads into the town. Of course, all cattle and sheep were driven into the market as obviously in those days there were no large stock lorries running about. Many of the public houses and some of the hotels, such as the Greyhound and the Swan accommodated the horses and the traps or carts were left in various yards or on the road outside the pubs. Cross Street particularly on the East side had many traps parked one behind the other practically the whole length of the road. All the pubs and hotels also had market rooms with an attendant to which shopkeepers could send parcels and goods bought by the farmers' wives who would collect them at the end of the day. In the cattle market every Tuesday there would be several buses, setting out at various times to Crickhowell, Longtown, Pandy, etc. Many a parcel of wallpaper I have delivered to a farmer's wife waiting for her bus in the market and been rewarded by a threepenny or sixpenny piece.

In September 1926 I left the Grammar School after obtaining my 'O' levels and entered the firm of C. Price and Son with a salary of fifteen shillings a week. My sister, Miss Dorothy Price, was an old hand, having joined the firm on 11 November, 1918. My father was partly crippled by arthritis, so we bought an Austin Seven with a collapsible hood.

1926 to 1932 was a time of great depression. This was far greater in its effect on the British people than the present day depression.

It was in the early 1930s that the Quakers came to this area and started two brave schemes in the town of

Brynmawr which must have had practically ninety per cent unemployment. Two factories were built, one to manufacture boots and shoes and the other for quality hand-made furniture. Today there are two factories in the town making boots and shoes, a direct outcome of the Quakers setting up a factory in the 1930s. Brynmawr furniture was a first class product made from Austrian oak.

Robert Price. (R.M.J.)

PETER COLEMAN

One thing I am very interested in is Abergavenny, especially the Abergavenny I knew as a child and growing up. I suppose there are many people who are older than me who have a far more comprehensive knowledge of the town and perhaps their memories are better, but I can recall some of the early days in my memory, days when horses and carts were the main means of delivery. I can remember the horses that were used by Burtons, the bakers. They had their stables in Lewis's Lane near the old Police Station, and in the morning they would get the horses from the stables and in a long train take them down Lewis's Lane, across the main street and on down Lion Street to the bakery which was quite a fine affair situated on the left hand side.

Lewis's Lane was quite a bustle of activity in those early days. There was a tremendous congregation of Irish cottages for Irish workmen. The cottages were small, very closely built one upon the other and filled in the area behind Hippo Campo and the site now occupied by the 2nd Abergavenny Scout hut and some of the space opposite. The little lanes and passages between the cottages were very narrow and there were a lot of people living there.

As what might be expected in the Irish community there was a Catholic Church and here there was St Stephen's Hall and St Stephen's Church. The hall was used by Herbie Davies, of Grofield Garages, as his MOT test building and the church itself now houses Dovers, the printers, and if you look closely inside you will find parts of the gallery still intact and the pulpit area or the sanctuary area of the church is now the office, and up until about 1983, there was a very fine brass chandelier suspended from the centre of the ceiling, but this became rather dangerous and it was removed by the present owners.

People like to think back to "the good times", but they were not all good times. There was a very interesting crash in Pen-y-pound when mail was coming down from Hereford towards Abergavenny and a run-away horse and cart careered across Park Road and crashed into it at Pen-y-pound, spilling mail and passengers all over the road. I think there were several fatalities.

Pen-y-pound itself is a strange name. When one looks at the signpost it seems to be Welsh with "Pen *hyphen* y *hyphen* Pound." In the old days it is said there was a pound there for stray animals. They would be rounded up in the town and taken to this pound and the redemption fee was a penny, hence the name "Penny Pound".

Among the things which used to amuse us very much were the milk deliveries, again by horse and cart, and I remember one dear old fellow who had his dairy in North Street. He used to have a very fine two-wheel cart conveying one great churn in the centre, and as a small boy I used to have a small churn that I could carry and the pint and half-pint measures were put in the churn. He would go into Tudor Street delivering to the houses in the courts. Nearly always these little houses had stable doors so that the top half could be opened and the bottom half remain shut. You would let yourself in and there on the scrubbed deal table would be a jug with a cloth over it and you could measure in the required amount of milk and cover it with the cloth and carry on with the delivery.

Nobody seemed to lock their doors in those days. Trust was the important thing. The milkman was quite a character. Nobody ever knew whether he wanted his horse to go fast or go slow because his cry would always be "Giddyup, Woa, Woa." As soon as his horse picked up speed he'd slow it down again.

Going away from Tudor Street through the old Town Wall into the town and Nevill Street, St John's Square, St John's Street, Chicken Street, Flannel Street, this was really a delight. These were little narrow streets with the atmosphere heavy from the activities taking place there. I remember working for a while for Hughes, the butcher, in Frogmore Street and every morning we would have to cut the meat from the bone and have a great pile to take to the Edwards' bakery in Flannel Street. There it would be transformed into beautiful meat pies to be sold in their restaurant and in their shop. What a delightful shop it was with its polished brass, oak and glass. In those days we had to keep our wits about us and I soon found out the time the doughnuts were being withdrawn from the oven, and if we coincided our meat delivery with the time the doughnuts were being prepared there would be a piping hot doughnut oozing with jam as a reward for taking the meat.

Frogmore Street.

Referring back to the Burton's bakery in Lion Street, one must mention the great mill opposite, Tuckers' Mill, one of the largest buildings in Abergavenny, a great big place with two towers fronting on to Lion Street to where the corn was delivered by dray, backing under the towers, taken into the mill and ground into flour. It was such a large mill and, incidentally, the first mill in the country to be powered by steam. It was a very wealthy place and a wealthy family who ran it. Most of the land around it in Market Street, Lion Street and part of the High Street was owned by Tuckers and the houses in Tiverton Place these were the houses that were built to house the workers at Tuckers' Mill, and tucked away right in the corner of Tiverton Place is a building still standing, although everything else has gone, which is a furniture stall. Part of it has been a Salvation Army Citadel and it has also been the home of the Freemasons. There it stands with a board above the door proudly pronouncing "Tiverton Place" when all about is vanished and the place is now a car park.

Getting back to the bakery at Redwoods. Oh, what a delight it was to walk past and smell the freshly baked bread and see the people working there and the little shop which used to be next to the Hen and Chicks with Potters the Tailors, a delightful little shop if ever there was one. Round the corner in Castle Street was Ben Taylor, the one-legged cobbler who spent half his time cobbling and the rest of the time sleeping off his hangovers.

In St John's Street close to the High Street was a little shop where there was basket-making. The door was always open and the basket maker would be working away there in the gloom of his little shop. He wasn't a very sociable man and children coming home from school who looked in at the door to see what was happening would find a mallet or something thrown at them. He didn't like being looked at at all.

We've just had a new fire station built in Hereford Road and a very fine establishment it is, but when the fire brigade was run by the town the fire station was located at the bottom of Market Street actually within the perimeter of the cattle market. There they had the rows of gleaming brass helmets and the old fire brigade – Ted Ball, Dick Horsington, Will Horsington and many people will remember – how they used to turn out with their big old-fashioned fire engine with fire escape strapped on the back, everything gleaming, everything bright, the whole thing absolutely wonderful.

In Lion Street, too, there was the Coliseum Cinema. How we used to queue there for the shows! When there was a good film on there would be so many people queuing to see it that they would have two distinct houses. Nowadays there is one showing a night and the place is half empty. The Coliseum was the old theatre of the town as well. I remember going backstage and seeing all the pulleys and the scenery, but I can only remember one slide show being held there, that was in the war time when a concert party arrived to entertain

people and the troops stationed in the area. Prior to the
Coliseum being a cinema there was a small cinema in
Park Road on the site of Tesco's garden centre. Films
were shown as the piano played away and the sound of
rain pattering on the roof only added to the
amusement.

Frogmore Steet. (R.M.J.)

Thinking back even further, where the cattle market is
situated was originally a field. The Guardians of the
Town in their wisdom decided to acquire the field and

make a cattle market out of it. There was one snag, however, because in this field was a building – the Bethany Baptist Chapel, so in order to acquire the field and use it for the purpose they intended they had the Baptist Chapel moved to a site in Market Street. The one thing which remained in the chapel which was from the original was the organ and that organ is still is use there today and is probably the oldest organ in the town.

Another thing which comes to mind is the way children of the town used to gather in the little lane behind Frogmore Street which used to run from Queen Street around the back of the shops along the course of the old Cibi and come out at the Herefordshire House. Unfortunately, this lane was never claimed as a public right of way and seems to have been lost because there are obstructions there now to prevent people walking that way. But this was a lane which we used as children many times and on New Year's Day early in the morning children of the town would gather at the back door of Scotts, the confectioners. There the old toffee works would be going full blast and every child in the town was given a mint lump about the size of his fist. It was made by Scotts and given away each year as a present to the children of the town, and if you were crafty you would claim your mint lump, go through the shop and then round the back to join the queue again to go through a second time. But the Scott family were very astute and would recognise most of the children and usually could tell if you were on the second way round.

When you go back to St John's Square and look at it now – there's the Post Office and the garden with the shrubs outside and big wide pavement and cornered by the Charles Price electrical shop and Annett's furniture shop and the tile centre and King's Arms Hotel and Old Court. Some of these places were there in olden times, but the Post Office sticks out like a sore thumb because it is not in the style of the square and the frontage of Charles Price's electrical shop, although very beautifully done, is reproduction. There was once next to that a mansion which made the square very small and triangular shape, really. It was bordered by the back of the Charles Price building and St John's Church, the Vine Tree Inn and the archway from the Vine Tree and St John's Square into St John's Street. And then there were houses with all sorts of funny images on the walls. Going under the arch which belonged to the Vine Tree Inn you entered a little street called Chicken Street where the houses overhung the pavement so that you could walk along in the dry even in the wettest of weathers.

There was a little Bookie. Of course Bookies were very usual, but this was a Bookie's Shop and he used to take his turn at being raided by the police, which was the system in those days, and when they were demolishing the arch and the houses in Chicken Street it was amazing that as they were removing the brickwork and plaster from this shop some beautiful old paintings and murals were discovered, but they were quickly destroyed by the machines that were clearing all the rubbish of the old in readiness for the brave new world that was going to be built on the site.

In the High Street where Cavendish Furnishing is now if you look above you can see all that remains of the old Greyhound Hotel which was a coaching house and down through the centre of the hotel was a passageway which ran from the back right through to the High Street, and leading off this passageway were the bars and the various rooms of the hotel, an hotel which was heavy in polished mahogany and brass, with great long bars, dining rooms, smoke rooms lounges and, right at the rear, a dance hall. I don't know how many dances and parties we attended at that place. It was the home of one of the old time dancing groups in Abergavenny and how we used to love to go there to dance to Joe Davies's orchestra. We thoroughly enjoyed ourselves.

The High Street itself was quite an amazing place. There was no through traffic through the town and in these days when people talk about pedestrianisation, traffic-free zones and all the rest of it, it is amazing to think that in days gone by the High Street actually finished at Market Street corner and there was a wall and a flight of steps to Cross Street, Cross Street of course being at a lot lower level than it is at the present day.

Of course, the old main street of the town was Tudor Street and it was only a matter of time before the shops moved across into the Cross Street, High Street, Frogmore Street area to become the centre of the town. At the bottom of Frogmore Street when the foundations were being put in for the Frogmore Street Baptist Church stepping stones were uncovered indicating that this was indeed a very wet area and people crossing from Grofield to get to the top end of the town or to cross over to the Hereford Road area had to use stepping stones at the bottom of Frogmore Street.

When one thinks of the past, nostalgia sets in and I remember that so often on nice days we would pack a picnic and go together in a family to St Mary's Vale. There there was an old iron pipe coming out from the stream where we could fill the kettle, light a fire and make the tea, have our sandwiches and buns and play games, and dam the stream and splash around in it – and it was cold. But the site was delightful and hundreds of people would go there. Now, of course, it's a National Park and National Trust and with these grand titles come the restrictions, what you can do and what you can't do – gates across the lanes, fences across the mountain, no fires, don't pollute the water.

Winter would come and one of our favourite slopes for sledging was in Delafield, now, of course, all built over with houses. But how we loved to get the sledges into Delafield and from the top of The Dingle sleigh down the slopes towards the Brecon road, great fun. And then when we went into King Henry's Grammar School, that was a great day.

There were no uniforms then because of rationing, but if you could get hold of an old cap you were the king of the school. Our cross country runs from the school used to take us into delightful countryside. We would run out from the school and up Avenue Road, past the cricket ground right the way through to the kissing gate at the top where it ran into Chapel Road and on up Chapel Road into the footpath at Chapel Farm and right the way up that footpath alongside the reservoir to the top and on across the stream with its old stone footbridge, up the other side to Sunny Bank and across the foot of the Deri, running along the grass tracks there and back across to Llwynu Lane, a delightful little lane which had its oak tree at the top end with a seat which people would sit on, especially at weekends when out walking. We'd go down the lane to Llwynu Farm. The farmer was a man named Johnson. We would vault his gate into the farmyard and see the old duckpond there with the ducks quacking around and the lovely old farmhouse, down through the barn and over another gate and into

the Llwynu fields, and we would follow the fields right the way down into the town, jumping the stiles until we reached the railway line which bordered Park Crescent.

The railway line seemed to tuck the town in very neatly. Nothing was built outside the railway. All the houses were contained within it and we'd cross by the little footbridge into Park Crescent. The last run into the school was along the pavement of Park Crescent and down towards the Convent and into the school where Percy Porter would be waiting with a tape across the road to see who would be the winners.

Holidays would come, and how we enjoyed them. They used to last for ever. One of the things we used to love to do was to get across to the Blorenge and climb the old tramway from Llanfoist right up to the exchange point half way up the mountain and follow the tramway around towards Pwll-du under the little tunnels, and they are still there today. Our imagination used to work wonders as we remembered how these horsedrawn trams would come round from the quarry at Pwll-du and the ironworks at Garndyrus, and they would come around to the middle of the Blorenge, and then by gravity the full trucks would come down and take the empty ones up. Some of the trucks would go to the canal where there was a boathouse at a place which we always called Barber's boathouse which is at present occupied by one of the Tod family.

As you came down the front of the Blorenge the stones which held the rails were still intact and still in place and you could put your finger into the hole in the stone which held the spikes which kept the rails in place. Just recently I returned to take some friends to see this old railroad but the road had almost disappeared and the stones which held the rails had disappeared also. Who would have taken them? Where have they gone? We don't know. Another branch of the tramroad crossed over the canal and came down to the bridge at Llanfoist over the River Usk and there was quite an important centre where limestone would be transferred to horsedrawn trucks and taken out on the old tramroad towards Tram Inn and on to Hereford. This early railroad was eventually replaced by another more up-dated steam track. The old stone bridge over the river was replaced by an iron bridge and it was widened to take double track, and steam engines were able to take all this stone, coal and everything else via Hereford into the Midlands to places where it was needed.

The canal itself was another delight because here was a place where as children we could enjoy ourselves. We learned how to row a boat, and although we did not have much money we would go along to Mr Rattigan at Govilon and chat to him and he would say, "I've got a group of people who want to go out in the boat and they don't know how to row. If you will take them out for an hour you can have the boat for half an hour, and so we would row a party out for an hour and then have the freedom of the boat for another half hour for ourselves, and this was really great. Occasionally there would be a mishap and many times I have seen people going home clothed in Mr Rattigan's Union Jack because their clothes were wet and they had perhaps to get to Brynmawr or to Nantyglo or one of these places above. The flags were always returned; dried and folded for the next incident which might come along."

There was another interesting feature about the canal and that was it abounded with wildlife. We used to love to go there with our nets and catch tadpoles and bring them back in jam jars and keep them in the garden at home until the tadpoles grew legs and the tails dropped off and they became little frogs. We never tired of this and every year we would watch the tadpoles grow and compare notes with our friends until the frogs appeared and then we would release them again near the canal. Another thing we used to catch in the canal were crayfish, fresh water crayfish, similar I suppose to the lobster or the sea water crayfish, but I have not seen a fresh water crayfish in the canal for many years.

There were many lines for the transportation of goods, coal and stone and one of the things which always amazed me was the fact that at Llanwenarth there was a section of track in the river with about half a dozen trams in the water as well. Just what that little track was doing there I have never been able to really find out, but it does make one wonder where all these different lines ran. Near the site where these trams were in the water was the shooting range, a great brick wall not far from the river where the Abergavenny Rifle Club used to spend their summers and where I myself spent many happy times with our neighbours and my father shooting at the targets. Quite close to the range was a memorial stone surrounded by little iron railings, a memorial to someone who had gone swimming at that particular point and had been drowned. And as the river moved its course so the erosion of the bank near the rifle range got under way and it was not long before the range and the memorial were overhanging the water, and then the railings, stone and the lot disappeared into the water. The erosion went on until it reached the shooting range itself and because there was no way for the footpath to go round it, a hole was knocked through the wall and a new footpath created. The shooting had stopped.

Bailey Park. This is still a feature of the town, a well used facility. Lots of people think that Bailey Park, as its name suggests, was given to the people of the town as a gift by the Bailey family. But this is not so. Again the Board of Guardians of Abergavenny, being quite far-seeing when the town was beginning to develop ribbon style along Hereford Road and ground was being taken up for building, decided to purchase the fields, the Priory Fields, as an open space for the benefit of the inhabitants of the town. They purchased it and the whole thing was endowed with funds and the place was given the name of Bailey Park, I suppose in honour of the Bailey family. It was certainly never a gift by the Baileys to Abergavenny.

Opposite the park was the Hereford Road School, the school which I attended as a boy. It was an amazing place with movable partitions and screens so that at school assembly the whole thing could be moved back to virtually make one great big open hall. Then the walls were returned to their proper position, dividing the whole thing up into classrooms. I had many happy days there and to see it now in its derelict form is a very sad thing. It had stared life as a Church School and was then, of course, taken over by the County and eventually was considered too old and too small, too inconvenient and too expensive. New schools were built and the old one was left derelict.

We moved from Hereford Road School to the Grammar School. We had to sit our eleven-plus, and well I remember the morning of the examination when we had to report to the Hereford Road School to get our marks and there we were given a ruler, pen, pencil and a rubber and we walked in a crocodile from the school to the grammar school to sit the examination. It was an experience. Hereford Road School was always the school which got most people through this examination.

I remember the teacher at Hereford Road School who took the scholarship class. He was known as old Daddy Parsons and he was a tough old character with a heart of gold. I remember as we were leaving the school to go across to the grammar school his final remarks to us were: "Don't get upset. Do your best. You can't do any better than that." That year out of the 30 odd places, 26 were taken by boys of Hereford Road School.

Grammar School Gate. (A.S.H.)

The Grammar School itself was a very fine building. Of course, the history of the Grammar School in Abergavenny goes back to the days of King Henry VIII and we all know the story of the Grammar School being endowed with the money from various tithes being allocated, how the standards of the school were to be administered by Jesus College Cambridge. There was a sum of money in those days of £50 a year to pay for the caretaker and the headmaster. That £50 a year is still payable and still comes in to the Grammar School – to King Henry School. But in the old building in Pen-y-pound we walked into the school hall and there were these two great black stoves, a couple of buckets of coal by each. They probably consumed more fuel than the locomotive *King George V* ever did on its run to Plymouth. The fires would be stoked up and the hall would shimmer, but it was never even warm, unless you were near the stove. One would look up at the wall to see the honours board – the honours gained by past pupils being kept up-to-date by the headmaster and his staff.

When the new school was founded as the basis for the new comprehensive, workmen moved into the old school at Pen-y-Pound to prepare it as a secondary modern school and one of their first acts was to rip down the honours boards and to dispose of them, and then to get out the paint and to paint the beautifully varnished pitch pine panels and doors and make the place a lot brighter for the new students who were going to enter into the place.

One of the things that I can remember very well at the old grammar school building was on VE Day, 8 May 1945. The news of the surrender of the German forces came through and everybody was cock-a-hoop. Oh, what a marvellous day! The celebrations went on late into the night. I can remember the record player – radiogram, as it was – wheeled out from the grammar school on to the front porch and records being played full blast while people danced in the grounds. And it was strange the following morning looking up at the school – right on top of the fancy ventilator which is on the roof was an old "gazunder" pot painted red, white and blue. Someone had scaled the building during the night and placed it atop the highest point. It was such an achievement! A local building firm was contracted to remove it and it took them two weeks to erect the scaffolding, retrieve the object and take the scaffolding back down. Still, there was an excuse.

Abergavenny, of course, like so many other local authorities, had its own gas works. These were in Merthyr Road near Llanfoist Bridge and it was quite an imposing building with two great gasometers and a great chimney which had a cowl over the top so that the flames could not be seen in war time. People would wheel their wheelbarrows there to load up with coke to keep the home fires burning, especially during war time – coke was cheaper than coal – and another of the by-products was tar. We would get a bucket of coal tar and we would be able to tar the roof of the shed; tar anything we wanted really. Tar was marvellous stuff.

Another use of the gasworks was its medical properties. Anybody suffering with whooping cough was taken to the Gas Works and allowed to walk around the galleries and inhale in great gulps of the sulphurous fumes which apparently gave great relief. Behind the Gas Works was the railway locomotive shed. The Old London North Western Railway and its headquarters for South Wales in Abergavenny. There was this great shed which housed 150 engines in its hey-day. Coal from Barry came down the line and was sent off to the Midlands by the old London Midland and Scottish Railway Company. It kept the railways

131

running for many years – Welsh steam coal was the best in the world.

The little line which wound its way up from Abergavenny to Merthyr – the old MT and A Line, Merthyr, Tredegar and Abergavenny. Many's the time I've caught the five to eight train, originally a little 2F long funnelled engine or locomotive, later to be replaced by a more modern "Mickey Mouse" 1200, 1201, 1202, 1203, 1204 series. "Mickey" used to take the two, sometimes three, carriages up the line to Merthyr. The carriages themselves were gorgeous. They were rich maroon with gold lining, outward opening doors which seemed to be set back into the doorway, shiny brass handrails and handles. They were all of the open-type carriage. You could walk between the seats and the luggage racks would be up over each seat, again in brass, the whole thing very ornately done.

It was unfortunate that when the line was transferred from the control of the Midland Region of British Rail to the Western Region of British Rail, it was discovered that these carriages were out of gauge and so they were sent to Caerphilly and they were burned and in their place they had the auto-cars, the push-pull variety with the door in the centre and the problems that this gave rise to, especially when there were platforms like Clydach, where the platform curved sharply. While you had doors at the end of the carriages like the old LNW carriages, people could step on and off without any difficulty. Now with the door at the centre of the carriage you found the door 12 or 18 inches away from the edge of the platform. And so a board had to be provided to bridge the gap so that people would not fall down.

But in travelling the line when the autumn mists were about was magic. We would leave Abergavenny Station with a shrill little whistle, down past the loco sheds, give another whistle, over the bridge over the Usk and up through Llanfoist, through the cutting, round by the old Llanfoist brewery and on to the steep line because the steepest part of the line was between Llanfoist and Gilwern where we gained height in the easier countryside ready for the haul through the Clydach Gorge itself, and as we climbed so we gradually came out of the mists of the morning into the clear blue skies and the sunshine, looking back towards Abergavenny one would see a sea of cloud and you were riding above it and the mountain tops would be sticking out like rocks in an ocean and the whole lot tinted pink by the morning sun, a view and memory not to be forgotten.

The sheds themselves – I've mentioned the immensity of them – had their wheel shops and their special machinery and turntables. We used to stop and watch the driver and fireman turning their loco before going for water from the water towers and calling up at the coaling station. And over in the corner of the loco yard was the shed which contained half the sand of Barry Island. What a delight it was to sneak over the wall and down into the shed to play in the sand . . . a wonderful time we had, till the loco would draw up and fill the sand boxes and we would be given a very curt "Clear off" and if we were too slow in moving a helping hand would appear across our backsides which would prevent us from sitting down at tea for many a day.

Then, looking across the town to the Little Skirrid, the smallest of the seven hills of Abergavenny – what a delight it was to climb the Little Skirrid. There was a well half way up where we always stopped for a drink of water. We would carry on up through the wood and it was just like going through the unknown land of North America. Occasionally we would come to a clearing and looking out would perhaps see a little of the town, plunging into the undergrowth again to make our way to the top. There right on the summit was a flagpole and the flag would be flown on high days and holidays reminding people of the town of their heritage, making everybody proud that they lived in such a place.

And, of course, the Little Skirrid being only half the size of its big brother, provided a wonderful vantage point, because the immensity of the mountains around was still there and the scale of the whole thing so exact. Looking down we were near enough to the town to pick out landmarks, the street where we lived, the house where we lived and the window of the bedroom. And Lady Herbert, a grand old lady in a grand house. No one could mistake Lady Herbert in her beautiful Lancaster car, quite an adept driver she was until in later life when perhaps with skills slipping away a little, the people of the house would discreetly phone the police and they would quickly move into the town and remove other motorists and obstacles in order that she would have a free run in, not because of privilege, but because of old age and the danger which might ensure otherwise.

The old house at Colebrook was a marvellous place

and, of course, in keeping with most other historic residences had its own bloodstained room and no matter how often the place was redecorated the stain came through. The story was of a duel to the death and the bloodstain was from the wounded knight.

Near to the house was the family chapel, all panelled in oak with a big tomb in the centre of the church, again a marvellous little place, and when the house chapel was eventually pulled down everything was stripped from them and sold.

Coming back from Colebrook to Abergavenny, and Abergavenny Castle, the castle which so many people remember nowadays for the Christmas Day massacre. Isn't it funny how people always remember the bad things? But, of course, the castle was an important residence and was used by Charles I on several occasions. In fact, the whole country was ruled from Abergavenny for a while by the King and it was at Abergavenny Castle that two Parliamentarians were brought before him, two prominent people of Abergavenny, when he was sitting in judgement and his advisers advised him to have these two men hanged because they were traitors. But the King was not like that and he released them with a warning and asked them to be good citizens and to go about their business and it was ironical that they rejoined the Parliamentary forces and no doubt were amongst the crowds in London at the execution of the very man who had let them off so many years earlier.

But as the castle fell into disuse and disrepair the Victorians picked up the pieces and created a walk along the walls, a wooden walkway or platform with marvellous views across the Usk valley. Now these have gone too and recently the Youth Opportunity people have been removing the stairways and preventing people from walking the walls anyway.

I was talking to a fellow not so long ago, who remembered his childhood when he did a lot of cycling. He said Abergavenny Castle he remembered so well because the caretaker there was a Miss Harding and she had her tea room and whenever he cycled from Pontypool to Abergavenny he always relaxed at the caste in Miss Harding's tea-room before returning to Pontypool. The Keep itself was a much more modern thing and in recent years had been used by Stephens, the caterers. Now it has been restored and will soon be used as an extension to the museum. Thank goodness, some things are going the way we would like to see them. Part of the castle was removed in 1939 in order to house troops of the British Army but I think that nobody knows its exact shape and design. Whereas at other castles mock-ups can be seen, Abergavenny remains one great mystery. Perhaps one day it will be excavated and all will be revealed.

For those who remember their childhood in this town the rope walk conjures up many happy memories. This was the lovers' walk down Lower Monk Street across the Gavenny and up Firs Road, past Coed Glas and over the footbridge over the railway and up into the fields and woods beyond. It was a regular place for courting couples and many is the time we have walked there and we've kissed and cuddled and taken part in this traditional ritual of the town. But the Eastern By-pass now slashes its way across the old walkway and one can no longer concentrate on one's partner in racing across the road to escape the speeding traffic.

There are many many features, some historical and some not so historical, and I wonder whether many people remember Molly Cox's chip shop at the bottom of Baker Street at the junction of Frogmore Street? This was a delightful place and Molly Cox's chips were known from one end of the country to the other. During the heavy days of the black-out there were always special arrangements for curtains to be placed across the doorway. One had to negotiate these to get inside, and once inside the hazy smoke from the chip fryer and the heady atmosphere there added to the delight of the chips when you got them and nothing has tasted the same since. In the black-out if you had a torch it had to be shielded, and cars, too, had their lights shielded. Then there was the American invasion of the town. American troops were camped in the Fairfield, Swan Meadows and all around the place.

They took over the Swan Hotel as their headquarters. The Swan Hotel was twice the size it is now. Vehicles would pull in under the verandah and spill out their passengers, and at the rear of the Swan stretching out towards Priory Lane was a great dance hall, and there were so many Americans using the place that they decided to shore it up with special pillars underneath. This really became the centre of activity for the town. At the end of the war the Americans left, compensation was paid to the owners and the place was sold and the new people decided to remove these pillars and the ballroom and rooms above it collapsed into a heap of rubble.

So, too, the Priory with St Mary's Priory Church with its wonderful monuments and all its historical connections. The troops were billeted in the Priory itself and at the end of the war it was sad that the compensation money that was paid by the government to the Vicar of St Mary's for any damage that might have been done to this beautiful old building was actually used to pay a demolition firm to demolish the whole lot. All that was left with now is the perimeter wall of the Priory building itself. How sad.

Old sheep barn, Castle Street.

Wool was a main occupation and industry in the town and there were two very important wool stores. There was Scott's wool store in Lower Monk Street and Skilton's in Mill Street and there was a great water wheel at Skilton's. There was a weir in the Gavenny river near Lower Monk Street and the water was channelled across the bus station yard in front of the Swan Hotel and under the road, under Tan House and down into the Skilton's wool yard. There I have stood many times and watched this great wheel being turned by the water. Part of the watercourse can still be seen, but there is no water in it nowadays and, of course, the wool stores have gone. At Scott's wool store they used

141

to wash the fleeces in the Gavenny and there was a special gap in the wall for them to do so.

Priory Gardens, retirement flats 1992. (P.N.H.)

Priory Park, June 1992. (P.N.H.)

Going back to the war time. A famous character visited the town – Field Marshal Montgomery. He came driving into the town in his jeep and I think the whole town and its neighbour were out to greet him. He signed the visitors' book, waved to the crowds and urged them to buy more Savings Certificates. Of course, his connection with Abergavenny was via his ADC who was William Crawshay of Llanfair.

Later we had the visit by the Queen. Her Majesty came by train and the station was transformed. She visited St Mary's Church, saw the monuments and commented favourably upon them. She came to the Town Hall and autographed the photograph of herself which still hangs in the mayor's parlour before leaving the town to go to Cwrt-y-Gollen Camp to re-open the camp which had been redesigned and virtually rebuilt. It was intended that her visit should be a very pleasant one by driving along the Blaenavon road with the Keeper's Pond and its marvellous views across the Usk Valley and then down the Eastern Valley, finishing up at ICI for tea. But, unfortunately, as so often happens here, it rained and rained and the mist came down and she could hardly see the pennant on the front of her car let alone any of the beautiful sights.

Seven Corners Lane

PAMELA HEATH

Fate seemed to play a very large part in drawing my husband and myself to Abergavenny.

In the 1960s we had thought of moving our factory from the Midlands to the Valleys. This did not materialise but Abergavenny proved to be the magnet that drew us to the town.

During the building of our house Abergavenny always seemed pleased to see us. We would leave the Midlands on a miserable wet day. Before we arrived in the town the sun would be shining on the Sugar Loaf and Abergavenny nestling in its basin of hills would hold out its welcoming arms.

Our house, opposite the Hill College was finally finished and on a beautiful day in June 1970 two large pantechnicons brought all our worldly goods from Solihull and with our daughter and two cats we moved house.

What a joy to be able to set off from our own front door for a delightful walk up the Deri or to St Mary's Vale. To see the sheep grazing in the fields and on the return journey to look over the town with the Town Hall roof green in the distance.

Market Hall. (A.S.H.)

146

In 1970 parking was not the problem it is today. One could park along the full length of Tudor Street, up to the time of the new Police Station being built. I can only suppose the Police did not want cars parked outside their front door to spoil their view, because very soon double yellow lines appeared and parking was banned. A pity as parking in Tudor Street made shopping very easy in the Market and the main streets. The Castle Street car park in those days was beautifully hap-hazard and one could drive around and pick a spot of one's choice, not like the Russian Roulette of the present day. Maybe, one day the Council will dig up a few kerbstones to enable us to get in and out without having to travel the circuitous one fifth of a mile.

Shopping in those halcyon days was fun. Basil Jones with his fascinating double doors which had to both be opened. If one tried to get in through one only it usually meant getting stuck in the middle. The beautiful fixtures and drawers of polished wood reminded one of the days long gone when rice and other commodities would have been stored there. I don't think I ever found out what was actually kept in those drawers. Hopefully these fixtures will not be lost and will be able to be seen in the delightful

Abergavenny Museum.

Fred Morgan in the High Street had turned into a self-service store and what one could not find in Basil Jones could usually be bought in the nearby shop.

The narrow part of the High Street with its small shops gave an interesting if impractical vista and it was a great shock when we were told the shops were unsafe and should be demolished. Almost overnight Kay-Dee, the super children's shop; the tiny sweet shop where one had to climb two, or was it three steps to enter and the small shop selling sewing-machines and pretty hats were all pulled down. Then came the time of the red girders. The name Red Square has stuck to this day. More's the pity!

Those girders seemed to be there to stay and stay they did for some years. However, eventually an agreement was reached and money was found to rebuild the dangerous wall and to re-open the High Street to the traffic which had meandered around Market Street all these years.

Alas this was not to be for long and very soon the area was pedestrianised. Now the pedestrians have to vie with the large lorries bleeping their way through the High Street and warning the walkers to get out of their way.

It was a sad day when the second cinema – the Coliseum closed its doors and now the nearest has to be Cwmbran or Newport. I suppose the advent of the video has meant the death knell to picture houses but perhaps we will be lucky enough to have a new cinema in the not too distant future.

Before "Red Square".

Travelling in the town when we arrived did not need a computer to tell us how to get from A to B. One could drive up Frogmore Street from the monument, stop at the traffic lights by Barclay's Bank to let the through traffic pass. Continue on a detour down Lion Street. On the return journey one could drive from The Angel Hotel, along the High Street into Frogmore Street and so back to the Brecon Road, stopping on the way to shop and pick up goods.

Angel Hotel, 1992. (P.N.H.)

The new precinct between Frogmore Street and Park Road has altered the old aspect of the town and the old stone houses in Queen Street are no more. How quickly we get used to the new and find it difficult to remember the old. The new Safeways store and car park very quickly took over a large part of the area.

I suppose that everyone now is in such a rush and Supermarket's have to be the answer. They do a very good job and save us wasting time talking to the shopkeeper. But, is it all for the best? I wonder?

We have been fortunate so far that although new housing has appeared it has not encroached onto the foothills of the Sugar Loaf. I sincerely hope it never happens.

The new trend of farm land turning into Golf Courses seems to be growing and new courses are being built between Abergavenny, Usk and Monmouth.

In the twenty years we have lived in Abergavenny the town has changed. Some may say for the better, some say for the worse but no-one yet has managed to dim the magic of the place. When the sun shines on the mountains and the surrounding countryside its beauty can compete with any other town in Britain.

SPORTS

APPENDIX 1

Association Football (Soccer)

Abergavenny Thursdays AFC was founded in about 1908 when shopkeepers and delivery boys organised play on their half-day – initially in Bailey Park at which time the Club entered the Hereford Thursday League. Before the Second World War – when Jack Ruther was President – with players such as Ray Floyd, Gus Doolan and Harold Bowen; and later Dai Croom, Pat Willard, Tom Fitzgerald and Harold Warren. At the end of the war, affairs were taken over by respective Chairmen George Mann and Joe Watkins – with assistance from the dynamic Vin Sullivan. At this time the Club made the bold move of acquiring the Penypound Ground and setting up grandstand and supporting facilities – and this earned the Club a Certificate of Merit from the Football Association of Wales, and during this successful period (mid-1950s) the Club won the League

Cup at Penydarren Park, Merthyr Tydfil. In 1959-60 under Manager Ray Lawrence the Club became League Champions. Enthusiasm dimmed in the late 1960s but the Club was saved by Stan Lang and returned to success by winning the Second Division Championship in 1975. After this the Club prospered with three teams under Manager Ray Warren winning promotion to the Premier Division. In seasons 1988-91 the team performed well in the Welsh National League and became league champions in 1990-91, also winning the Intermediate Cup by beating Mostyn at Llanidloes. Also in this season the Club reached the quarter finals of the Albright Bitter Welsh Cup – only losing to Barry Town after a replay. The Welsh F.A. recognised the Club by holding the Welsh Schoolboy Under 15 International – Holland v Wales – and the Welsh Under 19 Professional Youth Game between Wales and Norway at Penypound Stadium. The Club is currently achieving great success on the field.

Bowls

Abergavenny Bowls Club is the oldest in Wales and was founded in 1860. The Club originally played on a green at the Great Western Hotel – but interest waned towards the end of the nineteenth century but with the opening of the Avenue Road green in 1909-10 the Club blossomed and has since gone from strength to strength. During the period 1959-62 the Club had the "Famous Four" players who achieved many distinctions. They were Lyn Probert, Claude Stephens, Tom Griffiths and Albert Evans – and they won the News Chronicle Championship in 1959, W.B.A. Competition in 1960, they were British Isles Champions in 1961 and also won at The Empire Games in Perth, Australia in 1962. Lyn Probert captained Wales in 1963 and 1980 (and he had also been a fine cricketer). The Club won the Monmouthshire County Championship in 1985-86.

A thriving second club also exists in the form of the Bailey Park Bowls Club and this was founded in 1924 – and this resulted from the efforts of Major J.R. Jacob in negotiating the provision of the green. An outstanding player – John Anstey – was a Welsh International in years 1974-77 and 1982-85 – but sadly died in 1991. Also, Tom Griffiths, who achieved distinction with the Avenue Road Club, was a member of the Bailey Park Club.

Cricket

Abergavenny Cricket Club was founded in 1834 since when it has enjoyed a prominent place in the sporting life of the town – and the County. Within living memory such distinguished names as Dr. Tresawna, Major Jacob, R.W. Powell and Col. W.R. Lewis come to mind as outstanding players – but there were others too numerous to mention. There were cricketing families such as the Adams Brothers, Honeywell Brothers and the Robinsons and, in the immediate pre-Second World War days an outstanding player was G.N. O'Daly. After the war, Sidney Stock and Lewis White were two of the outstanding players. As always, the Shackleton family have been involved and the present President of the Club – Brian Shackleton – was a successful Captain from 1962-69 and 1974-75. However, the most successful player ever produced by the Club was undoubtedly Malcolm Nash (whose father and brother also played) who, after his early years with the Club in the 1960s, went on to join Glamorgan where he played in first-class cricket as opening bowler for the County team for many years and came as "near as a whisker" to winning a place in the England Test team.

In its early days, the Club played on one or two

grounds – including Bailey Park and Castle Meadows – but have been firmly established in their present most attractive ground at Avenue Road since about the time of the First World War. The Club has a fine reputation for organisation and hospitality and now hosts one first-class Glamorgan County game every season – drawing forth loud praise from many quarters – including one or two London journalists who have described the setting as the most beautiful of any cricket ground in the county.

Golf

The Monmouthshire Golf Club at Llanfoist was founded in 1882 and, as its name implies, was the first golf course in the County. The beautifully located site bordered by the River Usk was, in part, a racecourse up until the latter part of the nineteenth century. The Course – which boasts a historic old building (rather of Tithe Barn Type) as its Club House – was for many years a 9-hole course and the major step of extending it to a full championship 18-hole course was taken between the two wars, since when the Club has gone from strength to strength and, apart from great playing strength in individual and team championships, it now provides ever improving facilities, culminating in a special year of activities during the centenary year of 1992. Of all the fine players produced by the Club, perhaps the best of all is Iestyn Tucker who has won the Welsh Amateur Championship on many occasions – besides many other honours – and his is the current Captain of the Club during centenary years. Numerous new gold clubs are springing up in the County.

Hockey

Abergavenny Hockey Club was founded in 1897 and has always been among the strongest in Wales, upholding a strong hockey tradition in the town. For most of its life the Club has played at the Avenue Road Cricket Ground but in recent years it has moved to the all-weather pitch at the Abergavenny Leisure Centre. From the outset, Abergavenny produced distinguished players of international standard and in the early part of the century the Price brothers and the Jonathan brothers played for Wales. This was followed up between the wars when Collis Bishop – among others – won Welsh Caps. After the Second World War the Club enjoyed a period of outstanding success and – during the 1950s and 1960s the Club had several seasons when they remained unbeaten, playing the strongest first-class Clubs in Wales and the West of England. During this period, Harold Sharpe won many Welsh caps and Stanley Hall also achieved international status. However, perhaps the Club's most distinguished player was Dr. Bill Griffiths (now the Club President) who, besides winning many Welsh caps, also played in the Great Britain team in the 1948 Olympic Games.

Rugby

Abergavenny Rugby Football Club was founded in about 1880 and was, in fact, in being when the Welsh Rugby Union (the parent body) was formed. The Club – generally with two teams – has always been among the foremost second class Clubs in Wales – and particularly in Monmouthshire where it has won the Ben Francis Cup three times in recent years. The Club has produced a number of distinguished players – one or two having achieved international status. Derek Main was a fine international forward – and he also played for several first-class Clubs, including London Welsh, St Luke's College, Exeter and Devonport Services. Tony Wyatt also was an outstanding player – and was followed by an even more distinguished family – his son played for

Swansea and Wales and his daughter played for the Welsh Ladies.

The Club plays in Bailey Park where it has a large, well appointed Club House.

Tennis

The Avenue Road Tennis Club was founded shortly after the First World War when it had three grass courts in attractive surroundings in Pen-y-pound – which also included good club house facilities. At about the start of the Second World War a hard court was built and this process has continued in the post-war period so that the Club is now equipped with four hard courts of high quality. The Club has consistently produced good players and also has achieved success in inter-club matches. Until comparatively recently (when alterations to water courses etc., have been carried out) the courts were occasionally subject to flooding when the Cibi Brook overflowed. In fact, flooding has been known in the Avenue Road area (although this is no longer possible) and, during the Second War, the area now developed as a cul-de-sac of five or six houses was an army camp with huts occupied by ATS girls and locally, therefore, known as "The Attery" and the huts were flooded several times when the Kibi overflowed.

In Bailey Park there are excellent tennis courts which are available for use by the general public and – outside the town (at Pempergwm three miles away) is the Monmouthshire Croquet and Lawn Tennis Club which is old established with good facilities which now include hard tennis courts.

Abergavenny & Border Counties Show

The Abergavenny Horse Show – as it was called until comparatively recently – was founded in 1844 since when it has run continuously and successful as one of the major one-day agricultural shows in the country. In fact, for a short period after the Second World War, an experiment was tried of running the Show for two days but this proved unsuccessful – presenting many problems of organisation, stock accommodation etc., – and was quickly abandoned.

For much of its life – up until after the Second World War – the Show was held in Bailey Park and the adjoining Fairfield, but this gradually became quite impossible as the Show grew in size, and traffic, parking problems, etc. meant that a change had to be made. The Show then moved to its present location at Glebelands,

Llanwenarth Citra – approximately one and half miles from the town in a most beautiful setting in the heart of the Usk Valley. On this site the Show has use of an area more than three times the size of the Bailey Park site and obtains attendances of 15,000 at the Show.

The Show covers a wide range of interests and although based on the traditional stock exhibits – horses, cattle, sheep, pigs, etc. – there are also special sections for rare breed animals and large marquees containing horticultural and handicraft sections – and there is a large Dog Show as an almost self-contained unit. Each year there are special main ring attractions and in addition there is a wonderful range of trade stands which make for a wide variety of interests quite apart from the Show itself. There are numerous demonstrations of special arts and crafts.

The Show employs a full-time Secretary but apart from this, the greater part of the work in organising and setting up the Show, management on the day, etc. is carried out by volunteers from the agricultural community and other local organisations.

TWO CHURCHES
APPENDIX 2

St Mary's Priory Church

St Mary's, in the centre of Abergavenny, was originally built to serve the medieval priory. Little remains of the priory now, and the church itself was extensively restored in the 19th century. It is a large, handsome church, well worth a visit in itself. However, its principal claim to fame is the collection of effigies and monuments which it houses. Only one other parish church contains more, but those of Abergavennny extend over a longer period of time and are more varied in their construction. One of the earliest is of a Lady, probably Eva de Braose (d. 1256) who brought the Lordship of Bergavenny with her dowry when she married William de Cantelupe. The de Hastings family are well represented, wearing chain-mail and handsome moustachesl. One of the two Herbert brothers who lost their heads after the battle of Banbury in 1469 lies with his wife, Margaret. There is fine effigy of Sir

William ap Thomas, the first of the Herberts, with Gwladys his wife. She was the daughter of Sir David Gam of Llantilio Crossenny, who fought at Agincourt with Henry V.

Interior of St Mary's. (A.S.H.)

Later Monuments are not so war-like; there is fine Elizabethan tomb of Dr. David Lewis, First Principal of Jesus College, Oxford. There are a number of others. All these were local people, who with a great many others, chose to be commemorated in their parish church. Some of the monuments have been roughty treated in the past, and it is planned to raise money to get them expertly restored to some resemblance of their former dignified selves.

St Peters' Church, Llanwenarth.

This little county church has been a favourite of Abergavenny people for many years. Lying almost on the banks of the Usk, amid well watered meadows which also serve as a home for the annual Abergavenny Show, it is within easy walking distance of the town. It has a large churchyard, well stocked with enormous yews and other trees, and is an oasis of tranquillity reached by a narrow lane flanked softly flowing ditches.

A recent proposal to place a trunk road along this area was greeted with dismay by the Civic Society and many other people and organisations. Numbers of towns people have elected to be buried in the churchyard; it seems a terrible descretion to invade the peace of this charming spot for ever for the short-term advantage (if such exists) of a modern highway. If this is another of the so-called improvements of the 20th century that have afflicted Abergavenny, then it will be yet another monument to the insensitivity and disregard for public opinion that has been a continuing blight on the development of this modest but vibrant market town.

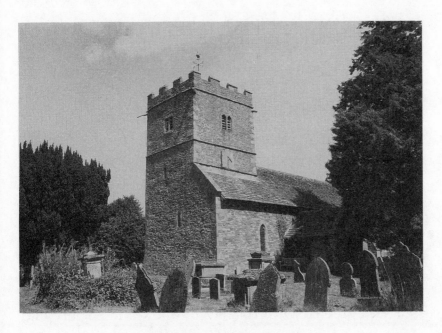

St Mary's Church. (A.S.H.)

ABERGAVENNY
STREET DIRECTORY

APPENDIX 3

A selection of pages of the Abergavenny
street directory in 1901.

Albany Road

(Right side from Western Road)

Brynhyfryd – Bishop, Joseph G, solicitor

St. Arvans – Williams, Alfred

Maisecmore – Gardener, Robert A

(Return)

Albany Lodge – Goulbourn, Ernest, assistant district superintendent, L. and N.W. railway

Ashfield – Reali, John Redmond Open-shaw, Inland Revenue officer, retired

Birchfield – Williams, William Reynolds, retired grocer

Albert Road

(Upper Side)

Avondale House – Harman, William Arthur, railway employee

LAUGHTON TERRACE

5.   Jones, Mrs Elizabeth

7.   Sheen, James, G.W. railway signalman

9.   Jones, Charles, G.W. railway signalman

Laburnum Cottage – Norris, James

Albert Villa – Davies, John

Victoria Villa – Widdowson, Mrs

Cobden Place – Edmunds, William H, commission agent

CAMBRIDGE TERRACE

33.   Gee, John, mechanical engineer

34.   Richards, James, railway employee

35.   Harborne, William, foreman painter

36.   Thomas, Robert, police sergeant

37.   Goode, Charles, attendant Monmouthshire Asylum

38.   Davies William, gardener

39.   Thomas, Thomas, railway signalman

(Lower side)

The Bungalow – Brooks, Mrs

Carlton Cottage – Dixon, William John, gardener

Alexandra Road

Hampstead Cottage – Charnock, Frederick, dispenser

24 Stanley, John, carpenter

Cummock House – Brooks, William T, railway signalman

Avenue Road

(Right Side from Penypound)

Hillbrook – Seargeant, Percy II, commercial traveller

Stanhope House – Phillips, Thomas Richard, Excise supervisor

Carlton House – Unoccupied

Lyndhurst – Tomkins, Thomas Harrill, auctioneer, etc

Baker Street

(Right side from Frogmore Street)

1.   Price, Albert John, mineral water manufacturer

3.   Edwards, George, timber faller

5.   Morris, Mrs Arabella

7.   Wager, Mrs

9.   Mattingley, Francis William, labourer

11.   Carpenter's Arms Beerhouse – Richards, Richard, proprietor

Mineral water works – Price, Albert John, proprietor

Conservative Club

Warehouse – Gwatkin Bros., painters etc

Warehouse – Corp, Robert, haulier

Warehouse – Morgan and Co., wool staplers

Horsington Bros., painters, etc

VICTORIA TERRACE

4.   Wibberley, Arthur

3.   James, David, accountant

2.   Tulle, George, pianoforte tuner

1.   Taylor, A, Brewer's clerk

Grofield Inn – Powell, William, proprietor

Carnegie Public Library

Holy Trinity Institute

Holy Trinity Church

Hygienic Bakery, Abergavenny   ESTAB. 1881

Nevill Street
(Right side from High Street)
1.   Pryer, Henry, chemist and druggist
3.   Cadle, Thomas Arthur, provision merchant
5.   Evans, H Hudson, dentist
7.   Steel, Dr William Dyne, medical officer of health
9.   Surgery – Drs. Steel, W.D., and Tatham, A .L.
11. Rother House – Gardener, Iltyd, solicitor, county court registrar
Offices – Gardner and Heywood, Messrs, solicitors
13. Ruther, Samuel J, fish and fruit merchant
15. Hathaway, H.S., dispenser
17. Burris, Phoebe, npholstress
19. Owen, E.V. and O.J., Minerva Printing Works
21. Delafield, Ernle, fishing tackle maker and general dealer
Tailors' workrooms – Daniel, C.J., tailor and draper
23. Bird, Edward J., railway clerk
Bird, Miss Lena, preparatory school for children
25. Jenkins, William Morris, maltster and leather merchant
27. Deleme, Harriet, funiture dealer
King's Arms Inn – Delafield, Thomas (brewer) proprietor
(Return)
34. Hudson, John haulier
32. Morris, Edward, marine store dealer
30. Smith, James Henry, general dealer
Bull Inn – Weekes, William, proprietor
26. and 27. Ruina
22. Meredith, William labourer
20. Jones, W.J., gardener
18. Price, Mary Jane, stay-maker
16. Price and Son, Charles, house decoratiors
14a. Gardner, George, machine ruler
14. Thomas, John, baker and confectioner
12. Palfrey, Thomas, excise officer, retired
10. Ardin, Madam Cecelia, dressmaker
8.   Hart, Hannah, London Registry Office
6.   Rowe, Frederick R., watchmaker
4.   Allen, Thomas currier

North Street
(Right side from Brecon Road)
Prospect House – Baron, Thomas loco engine driver

Brynhyfryd – Evans, Mrs Caroline
10. Lane, William, head ostler
12. Green, George, railway signal inspector
14. Springfield Cottage – Parry, Walter, attendant Monmouthshire Asylum
16. Tennant, James T, railway clerk, retired
18. Watkins, Mrs Elizabeth
24. Green, Joseph, permanent way inspector
26. Blackmore, Henry loco fireman
28. Symonds, CL, cycle agent
Belle Vue Beerhouse – Cole, Herbert, bootmaker
32. Jones, Mrs Sarah
34. James, David Lewis, coal merchant
36. Shore, John, railway brakesman
38. Kewstoke – Gregory, Mrs Mary L
40. Brynderri – Townsend, Robert, solicitor's clerk
42. Williams, Mrs Ann
44. Gardener, Samuel, fitter
46. Griffiths, Mrs Marian
Bedwelty Villa – Howells, Absalom, commercial traveller
1.   Tredegar Villas – Eyers, Edward, railway auditor
2.   Tredegar Villas – Corp, Robert coal merchant and general haulier
Rose Villa – Lewis, Henry, retired publican
99. Vaughan, Edwin, timber faller
97. Durose, Thomas, railway clerk
95. Empty
(Return)
Scarborough Place – Palmer, Benjamin, railway blacksmith
93. Gates, Thomas, locomotive engine driver
91. Woodhouse, William, platelayer
89. Sheen, Charles, stonemason
87. Walkley, William, locomotive fireman
85. Bishop, William, butcher
83. Davies, Charles, locomotive fireman
81. Mergan, William, butcher
69. Powell, Miss Amelia
67. Bruton, Fred, hay-cutter

Hygienic Bakery, Abergavenny   ESTAB. 1881

48. Williams, John, foreman locomotive cleaner
50. Dennis, Mrs Phoebe, tailoress
52. Fitzgerald, Patsy, labourer
54. Maidment, William, labourer
56. Francis, Charles, locomotive steam riser
58. Gibbons, John, blacksmith's striker
60. Thatcher, Robert, locomotive engine driver
62. Jones, Albert, locomotive engine driver
64. James, John, Gas Works' stoker
(Return)
71. Thomas, William, labourer
69. Thomas, John, labourer
67. Morgan, Edgar, labourer
65. Phillips, Fred, journeyman tailor
63. Griffiths, William, labourer
61. Stanton, John, labourer
59. Knight, Mrs Ann
57. Fitzpatrick, John, journeyman tailor
43. Morris, James, carpenter
41. Sadler, James, loco engine driver
39. Evans, George, labourer
37. Webb, George, labourer
29. Sadler, James, carpenter, retired
1. Norman, Edwin, L. and N.W. railway gate keeper

Castle Street

(Left Side from Castle Street)
Castle House – Holding, Daniel, Warden
Castle Lodge – Thomas, John, caretaker
29. Goode, Thomas, postboy
31. Hill, David, farrier
33. Davies, Mrs Mary
35. Pritchard, the Misses, dressmakers
37. Cooke, Joseph, fitter
39. Denbury, Morgan, groom
Castle Street Schools
41. Luther, Martin, waiter
41. Luther, Madam, dressmaker
43. Norgrove, Alfred, journeyman baker
45. Thomas, Mrs Mary Ann
47. Walker, Walter, postman
45. Thomas, Samuel, brewer's drayman
49. Crompton, Fred, journeyman mason
50. Fudge, Robert, coachman gardener
52. Tatham, Dr A.L.

54. Radford, Miss A .E., schoolmistress
56. Watkin, William, mason
58. Old Duke Inn, by James Davies
59. Roberts, Mrs Lucy
61. Nicholls, Thomas, chimney sweep
63. Morgan, Mrs Adelaide
Warehouse – Vacant
Warehouse – Cadle, Thomas A
Old Court and grounds – Vacant
65. Norton, Joseph, bootmaker
66. Norton, Laurie, grocer
(Return)
34. Hudson, John, haulier
20. Hall, Emily Catherine, district nurse
18. Parry, Charles, journeyman painter
16. Bowen, Rev Thomas, Congregational minister
12. Pitt, George, grocer's carter
Wesleyan Chapel
Warehouse – Davies, William
Congregational Church
Congregational Hall

Chapel Road

(Left side from Brecon Street)
BRIDGE COTTAGES
1. Booth, John, looo engine cleaner
2. Green, Edward, loco fitter's mate
3. Jones, James, coachman
3a. Jackson, Joseph, L. and N.W. Railway labourer
5. Jones, Edward Arthur, L. and N.W. Railway porter
7. Rutter, – loco engine clearer
9. Morgan, Ernest, farrier
11. Watkins, George, loco fireman
13. Shaw, Joseph, chimney sweep
15. Barlow, John, printer's compositor
17. Marshall, Saml., foreman L. and N.W. Railway, telegraph department
19. Brown, Harriet, dressmaker
21. Parry, John, coal merchant
23. Llwellin, Maria (Box Cottage)
25. Sullivan, Bertha (Holly Cottage)
27. Light, Albert, storekeeper L. and N.W. Railway
29. Meadows, George, cowman
31. Richards, Mrs Ellen
33. Webb, Alexander, corn merchant's foreman
35. Davies, Harry, coachman
37. Berry, –
38. Jones, James, butcher's foreman
    Jones, Mrs, dressmaker

41. Peake, Edward, milkseller
43. Nevill, Mrs Marion
45. Window, George, platelayer
47. Archer, George, gardener
Sparchford Villa – Chamberlain, Thompson
Dellury Villa – Fry, Col. Sergt. Alfred, Instructor Local Vol. Co.'s
Cedar Place – Morris, Samuel
The Laurels – Reynolds, Arthur, commercial traveller
Inglewood – Unoccupied
Rose Cottage – Dennis, Miss

MINA VILLAS
1. Price, J.A.G., solicitor's clerk
2. Rogers, T Allan, school teacher
Poplar Villa – Dolling, Thomas
Derristone – Johnson, E.A., architect
Rock Villa – Tong, Wallace J, auctioneer and estate agent
Glancibi Grange – Seargeant, Henry, printer and bookbinder
(Return)
The Chain – Baker-Gabb, Richard
Chain Cottage – unoccupied
The Rowans – Cotton, Chas. O S, L. and N.W. Railway engineer
The Rocklands – Wilson, Mrs Emily G
Ashley Villa – Rosser, William, school teacher
Clyne Villa – Mansfield, F J, railway clerk
The Home of Flowers – Pitt, Henry, proprietor
Tytan Villa – William, Mrs Mariaanne
Stanhope Cottage – Woollans, Mrs Caroline
Clevedon Cottage – Kirby, W.P., loco engine driver

STANHOPE VILLAS
1. Farquhar, James Hervey, solicitor
2. Tonkin, Mrs Elizabeth
30. Tonkin, Alfred Ernest, grocer
26. White, William E, tailor
24. Powell, James, railway passenger guard
22. Moseley, Evan, painter, Monmouth Asylum

Chicken Street
1. Lewis, Amos, shoemaker
2. Bevan, R W, hairdresser
3. Woodhouse, M A, fishmonger and fruiterer

Clifton Road
(Left side from Ross Road)
Burford Villa – Jeffreys, William timber valuer
Langstone Cottage – Morgan, George, park keeper

CLIFTON VILLAS
2. Wibberley, Percy, auctioneer's clerk
1. Maddocks, Cartwright, grocer's foreman
(Return)
21. Shephard, Frederick, railway employee
19. Llewellin, Wallace, assistant town clerk

Commercial Street
(Left side from Brecon Road)
24. Brock, Mrs Sophia
25. Woodley, John, labourer
26. Edwards, Edwin, woodcutter
27. Thomas, George, carter
28. Griffiths, Mrs Emma
29. Prosser, William, cab-driver
30. Walters, Edward, platelayer
31. Powles, Henry, brewer' assistant
32. Sevenoaks, Albert, brewers' carter
32a. Davies, Mrs
33. Williams, John, sawyer
34. Keyte, Mrs Mary Ann
35. Davies, Mrs Elizabeth
36. Davies, John, labourer
37. Morgan, Mrs Elizabeth
38. Tickle, William, loco fireman
39. Hall, William, labourer
40. Morgan, John, hot water fitter
(Return)
Garden Cottage – Tranter,William, railway employee
Rosehill Cottage – Williams, E .J., retired colliery manager

Cross Street
(South side)
1. Bank House – Jone, Frederick Trevor, draper
2. Bevan, William and Pritchard, Alfred, ironmongers
3. Wheatsheaf Inn – Price, Samuel, proprietor
4. White Swan – Alden, T. G., proprietor
5. Morgan and Evans, Messrs, grocers and dealers
6. Allcott and Co., Messrs, ironmongers

A trial order solicited.

102. Jenkins, Mrs maternity nurse
103. Moss Cottage – Spillane, Thomas, railway engine fitter
98. Fern Cottage – James, Edwin, loco engine driver

FITZROY TERRACE

94. Morgan, Mordecai, loco fireman
92. Smith, James, telegraph wireman
90. Davies, Owen, loco fireman
88. Bevan, Robert, railway brakesman
86. Williams, Edward, loco engine driver
84. Matthews, Henry, loco engine driver
82. Davies, Abraham, railway brakesman
80. Slade, Thomas, railway porter
78. Mansfield Place – Jones, Edmund, mason
76. Vaughan, Mary Ann, grocer and confectioner
74a. Hall, John, railway parcels van

FROME PLACE

74. Giles, Tom, shoemaker
72. Powell, Alfred John, railway carpenter
70. Mills, Fred, telegraph wireman
68. Tranter, Daniel, loco fireman
69. Prosser, John, railway goods checker
64. Williams, Frank, gardener

MONTAGUE TERRACE

60. Parker, William, railway brakesman
58. Jones, T .W., retired publican
56. Challenger, Tom, insurance agent
54. Phillips, William Charle, printer's compositor
52. Matthews, Charles William, railway carpenter
50. Cooke, John, painter

St. John's Lane

Warehouse – Edwards, G.R., furniture dealer
Warehouse – Tutt, J, grocer
Warehouse – Cadle, Thomas A, grocer
Warehouse – Empty

St. John's Square

4. Empty
6. Pratricum, Mrs Mary
8. Burrows, Thomas
10. Parry, Mrs Mary
(Opposite)
9. Higgs, William, railway brakesman

11. Harpur, Mrs Louisa

St. John's Street
(Left side from High Steet)

1. Jones, Sarah A, china stores
12. Jones, Edward, journeyman tailor
10. Jenkins, Frederick
8. Empty
6. Thomas, Ernest, grocer
(Return)
The Vine Tree – Harries, Janet A, proprietress
Warehouse – Thomas, Ernest, grocer
Welsh Flannel Warehouse – James, Richard George
Masonic Hall, Freemasons' (Old St. John's Church)

St. Michael's Road

Warehouses Messrs C.H. Sayce and O.J. Williams

Trinity Street
(Right side from Baker Street

1. Jones, J.S., insurance and general agent
3. Day, William, gardener
5. Jones, Rees, journeyman tailor
7. Watkins, Miss Emma
9. Neville, Henry, relief locomotive engine driver
11. Walsh, Richard, harness maker
13. Morgan, Miss Leah
15. Philips, Richard, labourer
17. Roberts, George, plasterer
19. Crowley, Mrs Mary
21. Empty
23. Evans, William, stonecutter
25. Holland, James, painter
27. Lewis, Lewis, labourer
29. Morris, William, coal haulier
31. Morgan, William, timber haulier
32. Morris, Thomas, labourer
33. Hill, Harry, painter
(Return)
16. Bevan, John, journeyman tailor
14. Stanton, John, labourer
12. Keylock, George, labourer
10. Webb, James, Gas Works'stoker
8. Roberts, James, railway platelayer
6. Lewis, Mrs Jane

And all kinds of Brown Bread

171

4. Bryant, Barnard John, printer's compositor
Trinity Villa – Restall, Henry George, vaccination officer, assistant overseer, collector of local rates and of imperial taxes

Tudor Street
(Right side from Castle Street)
King's Arms' Brewery – Delafield, Thomas, proprietor
1. Powell, Mrs Ann

COURT A
1. Iron, Tom, labourer
3. Mansfield, James, labourer
5. Empty
4. Robertson, James, journeyman painter
2a. South, William, wood-cutter
2. Thomas, William, labourer
3. Watkins, John, chimney sweep
5. Registered Common Lodging House – Watkins, John
7. Richards, Samuel Morgan, timber merchant

COURT B
1. Wilson, John, labourer
2. Wyatt, James, labourer
3. Badham, Mrs Eliza
4. Davies, William, labourer
9. Hollis, Benjamin, mason's labourer
11. Evans, Tom, mason's labourer

COURT C
1. Jomes, Annie, laundress
2. Young, Joseph, drainer
3. Jones Edward, labourer
4. Dodd, Robert William, coal hawker
5. Green, James, labourer
6. Evans, John, labourer
Blue Belle Inn – Winter, E H, proprietor
17. Registered Common Lodging House – Elizabeth Griffiths
Old Baptist Chapel – Disused
19. Registered Common Lodging House – Elizabeth Griffiths
21. Pritchard, William, labourer
23. Griffin. Dick
25. Reynolds, George, labourer
27, 29 Knight, Thomas, marine store dealer
31. Empty
33. Taylor, James, labourer
35. Registered Common Lodging House – Toland, George

39. Havard, John, labourer
Cross Keys Inn – Adams, Jane Ann, proprietress
43. Finn, Cornelius, labourer
45. Regan, John, labourer
47. Lynch, Patrick, labourer
49. Roberts, Mrs Sarah
51. Honohan, Andrew, railway labourer
White's Yard – Ruins
61. Martin, Mrs Catherine
63. Roach, Mrs Mary
65. Watkins, Mrs Mary
Foresters' Arms – Vest, Herbert, proprietor
69., 79. Ruins
81. Walton, Thomas, labourer
83. Donovan, John, second-hand dealer

LAUNDRY PLACE
1. Gibson, Frederick, plumber
2. Ralph, George Henry, wheelwright
3. Pritchard, Leonard, baker
4. Harrhy, William, warehouseman
5. Jayne, Aaron, grocer's assistant
6. Symonds, Frank, groom gardener
7. Pettitt, Thomas, railway labourer
8. Holland, Jeremiah, mason
(Return)

LEWIS'S COTTAGES
1. Mace, Mrs Susan
7. Conolly, Mrs Catherine
9. Finn, John, labourer
10. Baldwin, John
8. Lowe, Henry, labourer
6. Empty
4. Simmons, Mary
2. Emmett, Caroline
94. King, Walter, railway warehouse-man
92. Went, Thomas, gardener
90. Price, Joseph
88. Warrinder, Mrs Eliza
86. Powell, Edwin, loco engine driver
84. Bail, David William, carpenter
82. Brown, George, labourer
80. Blackmore, Willliam George, gardener
78. Pugh, Israel, carter
76. Rathbone, Frederick, railway plumber

COURT F
Morgan, Thomas, carter

All orders promptly attended to.

2. Corbett, Thomas, labourer
3. Taylor, Charles, labourer
74. Powell, John, labourer
72. Jones, Mrs Annie
70. Wyatt, John, plasterer
68. Minton, Mrs Elizabeth
66. Watkins, Mrs Hannah
62., 64. Hatton. James, carpenter
60a. Lynch, Jeremiah, labourer
60. Williams, William, greengrocer, etc.
58. Berry, Mrs Susan
56. Conolly, Garrett, labourer
54. Lynch, Ellen
52. O'Grady, William, gas works' stoker
50. Hill, William, tiler and plasterer
48. Conolly, Patrick, labourer
45. Registered common lodging house – Morgan, Godfrey
44. Registered common lodging house – Breakwell, George

COURT D
1. James, labourer
3. Bevan, Daniel, shoemaker
5. Macarty, John, labourer
7. James, Robert, carter
9. Welsh, Patsy, labourer
11. Macarty, Dennis labourer
13. Davies, Mrs
14. Seaborne, Joseph, blacksmith
12. Hodges, Charles, labourer
10. Meade, Patsy, labourer
8. Rogan, Mary
6. Morgan, William
4. Pugh, Samuel, woodcutter
2. Griffiths, Richard, hawker
42. Breakwell, George, gardener
40. Empty
38. Conolly, John, labourer
36. Jones, John, plasterer
34. Adams, Richard, fish curer
32. Deaves, Isaac, baker and confectioner
30. Harris, William, labourer
28. Davies, Elijah, dealer
26. Registered common lodging house – Toland, George
24. Reed. Edwin, Borough Bakery
Old Volunteers' Hall, ruins
20. Empty
18. Davies, Elizabeth, confectioner

16. Registered common lodging house – Griffiths, William
14. Registered common lodging house – McMullan, Mary
12. Smith, Frederick, tobacconist, etc
10. Harris, Frederick, blacksmith
Tudor Arms – Morgan, Lewis proprietor
6. Graham, Alfred, tiler and plasterer
4. Morgan, William, fitter
2. Madden, Jerry, china rivitter

Union Road
(Left side from Merthyr Road)
29. Young, John Henry, colliery foreman
31. Watts, David William, loco fireman
33. Blanche, Edward, mason's labourer
35. Vaughan, Samuel, milkseller
39. Shaw, William, loco engine driver
41. Hall, Frank, coppersmith
43. Rouse, William, labourer
45. Bevan, George, gas works' stoker
47. Owers Emma
49. Lewis, Frederick Charles, loco cleaner
51. Evans, William, accountant clerk
53. Albion House – Price, John, gardener
55. Aston Beerhouse – Delafield, Miss Ada C.M.
57. Lewis, Albert, loco fireman
59. Evans, Edgar, railway platelayer
61. Dale, Thomas R, railway storekeeper
63. Griffiths, William, gardener
65. Morgan, Mrs Hannah
67. Pulleyblank, John, railway coalman
Hancock, Ann, maternity nurse
69. Webb, George, telegraph linesman
71. Booth, Charles, railway coalman
L & N.W. Railway Engine Sheds
The Manor Lodge – Nash, Edward, gardener
(Return)
48. Merriman, Thomas, loco engine driver
46. Davis, William, miller's foreman Abergavenny
Union Workhouse – Brown, W, master
40. Davies, John, bricklayer
38. Riley, George, railway yardman
36. Cooke, William, relief loco engine driver

EMMIE'S COTTAGES
1. Hiley, Mrs Jane
2. Jones, John William, insurance agent
3. Blizzard, George, railway platelayer
Park Cottage – Edwards, alfred, railway guard

Everybody praises it.

173

Redwood's Bread is unsurpassed

UNION TERRACE
1. Dodd, Ebenezer, farm bailiff
2. Prosser, Sarah J
3. Barton, – gardener
4. Hurst, Thomas, mechanical turner
5. Walters, Henry, carpenter
6. Stacey, Arthur, insurance agent
7. Johns, John Thomas, carpenter
8. Smith, James, tailor
4. Pugh, David, bootmaker
3. Clavey, James
2. Jones, David, Gas Works' stoker

Victoria Street
1. Davies, Walter, butcher
1a. Cooke, David, draper and tailor
3. Powell, Henry, carpenter
5. Wycherley, Albert, foreman painter
7. Hampton, Andrew, picture famer
9. Jones, James, relief loco engine driver
11. Brinkwood. William, loco fireman
13. Hill, Elijah John, railway gate keeper
15. Davies, Charles, butcher
17. Davies, Ellen
19. Oakley, Elizabeth
21. Palmer, Thomas, railway pensioner
23. Lewis, James, stationary engine driver
Lewis, William, gardener
25. Williams, Jane
27. Childs, Emily S
29. Jones, Elizabeth
31. Barnes, Thomas, shoemaker
33. Davies, William Henry, sewing machine agent
35. Davies, John, loco fireman
37. Taylor, Mrs Alice
39. Garraway, Francis, labourer
41. Roberts, David tiler and plasterer
43. Gunter, James, firewood seller
43a. Green, William, loco engine driver
45. Morgan, Tailiesen, milk seller
45a. Hooper, Edward, carpenter
47. Thomas, James, collier, Borough Bandmaster
47a. Kennard, Herbert, labourer
49. Brown, Jane E
51. Jones, Richard engineer
Mount Pleasant Inn – Dunn, Joseph proprietor

(Return)
62. Jones, William Watkin, carpenter
60. Morgan, Matilda
58. Morgan, William, grocer's carter
56. Parsons, Charles, carpenter and joiner
54. Jenkins, William, painter
52. Willis, William, bus driver
50. Jones, William, railway labourer
48. Lewis, John gardener
46. Lowe, Rebecca
44. Jones, Margaret
42. Murphy, Michael, labourer
40. Mead, John, labourer
38. Lewis Leonard, labourer
36. Higgins, Frank, railway platelayer
34. Stephens, George, loco engine driver
Victoria Street Schools
32. Matthews, George, railway brakesman
30. Dunn, Elizabeth
28. Griffiths, William, steam-roller driver
Beaufort Arms (Beerhouse) – Denner, John M, proprietor
24. Davies, John, loco fireman
22. Hemmings, William, brewer's assistant
Primitive Methodist Chapel
18, 20 Powell, Charles, baker and confectioner
16. Hill, Margaret
14. Hulson, Harry, plumber and painter
12. Parry, Thomas, foreman carpenter
10. Price, Emily
8. Herring, Robert, Council gas fitter
6. Michael, George, railway signalman
4. Ross, Ivor John, coal merchant and haulier
2. Roberts, David
Carnegie Public Library

Western Road
(Right Side from Chapel Road)
Western House – Evans, James A, railway clerk
Bryn Redyn – Hodgens, Benjamin Edgar, solicitor
Clunmore Villa – Sifton, T Headland, Headmaster, King Henry VIIIth Grammar School
Hollyhurst – Corner, Dr, Clerk in Holy Orders
Vanior – Empty
Fern Villa – Cooke, Rev T E Cozens, Baptist minister
Ellerslie – Cunliffe, Arthur M, solicitor

It is delicious and made daily

174

Unicorn Inn – Rogers, James, proprietor
26. Davies, Sarah
24. Britton, William, mason
22. Murphy, John, labourer
Mill Street Mission Room
Fellmonger's Yard (disused)
20. Sirrett, George, sawyer
18. Watkins, Mrs Elizabeth
16. Hill, Eliza
14. Davies, William, gardener
12. Dolphin, Rachel
10. Jones, Jane, grocer
8. Bevan, Eliza
6. Meredith, William
Warehouse and Stable – Duggan, Mary E
Millbrook House – Poole, Mrs Emma

Monk Street
(Right Side from Cross Street)
5a. Hudson, Henry, wine merchant's manager
5b. Office – Price, James, contractor
7. Roberts, John, saddler
9. Roper, Frederick John, carter
St. Mary's Chambers – Johnson, Edwin Arthur, architect
St. Mary's Chambers – Bishop, Joseph George, solicitor
Inland Revenue Offices
Church Room (over)
15. Lewis, George, brewer's drayman
Warehouse – Richards, Samuel Morgan, timber merchant
Priory Private Hotel – Davies, Samuel proprietor
St. Mary's Church
21. Coach Factory and House – Probert, Samuel
22. National Telephone Co. Call Office
23. London Hotel – Jenkins, Miss, proprietess
24. Alderton, Walter, baker and confectioner
25. Russell, William, railway fuel inspector
26. Cartman, John, assistant school master
27. Edwards, Mrs Elizabeth
28. Evans, John, grocer's carter
29. Williams, Charles, grocer
33a. Fort, Alfred, carpenter

COURT B
1. Jones, Thomas, carpenter
2. Preece, Joseph, labourer
3. Burrell, William, mason's labourer

35. Watkins, Matthew, plasterer
37. Gough, William, coachman
(Return)
40. Powell, Mary Ann, grocer
    Powell, Edgar, house decorater
38. McMaster, Margaret, private school for children
36. Chief Constable's Office – Kynch, William, Deputy Chief Constable
34. Gentlemen's Club
32. Gabb, R Baker, and Walford James Berry, solicitors
30. Davies, Dr. Samuel Hugh Rattray
28. Humfrey, Miss Lucy C
Hope Cottage – Holland, William, postman
Offices – James, J Gethin, land surveyor
26. House and Offices (unoccupied)
24a. Carr, William Robert, teacher of music
24. Williams, Thomas (sexton), builder
22. Rutherford, John Thomas, Town Clerk
20. Watkins and Son, William, bakers and confectioners
18. Davies, Frederick James, tailor
16. Williams, Miss Mary
14. Griffiths, Thomas, plumber and painter
12. Brown, Robert, G.P.O. linesman

MAGNOLIA TERRACE
1. Medlicott, Henry, railway brakesman
2. Tomkins, William, waggoner
3. Walters, Evan, mason's labourer
4. Jeffreys, Miss Catherine
5. Perks, John, painter
6. Unoccupied
10. Magnolia House – Charles, Mrs Ada Jane
8. Gwyther, Henry, boot repairer
6. Laburnum House – Goatman, Walter George, grocer
4. Edmunds, Miss L H (Ye Old Priory Cafe)

Monmouth Road
(Right side fom Cross Street)
Tanhouse – Under repair
Tanneries (disused)
Harrison, Abraham W, mechanical engineer and motor expert
Cycle Works – Symonds, Charles L
Bridge End Inn – Rosser, George, proprietor

Everybody praises it.

BIBLIOGRAPHY

The ABERGAVENNY CIVIC SOCIETY has been fortunate in that it has received copies of the comprehensive Bibliography of Gwent compiled by the Gwent County Library Service, with the addition of a supplement of additional items pertaining to Abergavenny. This is a compilation of material available up to 1986, and includes items of historical interest such as catalogues of sale of important properties, regional surveys, archeological and architectural papers, books, maps and planning proposals.

Most of the material is held in various Gwent County Libraries, but some relating to Newport is held at the Newport Reference Library. Those wishing to research a particular aspect of Gwent (or Monmouthshire!) history should in the first instance apply to the Bibliographical Services, Gwent County Library HQ, County Hall, Cwmbran NP44 2X1. They can then be directed to the particular County Library in which the manuscript is held and it will be there that it will be available for study.

Members of the Civic Society can of course consult the Bibliography themselves. It is held by the Hon. Secretary.